Challenges Facing
the
Orthodox Church Movements
in
East Africa

A Historical and Canonical Survey

Elekiah Andago Kihali
(Rev. Dr. Archimandrite Anastasios)

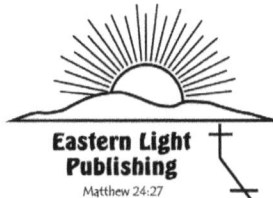

**Eastern Light
Publishing**
Matthew 24:27

Eastern Light Publishing, LLC

SHERIDAN, WY

Eastern Light Publishing, LLC.
30 N. Gould Street, Suite 2302
Sheridan, WY/82801
www.easternlightpublishing.com
Email: info@easternlightpublishing.com

Challenges Facing the Orthodox Church Movements in East Africa - 1st ed.
By: Elekiah Andago Kihali.

ISBN 978-1-949940-15-2 (Paperback Version)

This Present Work Was Adapted From a Thesis Presented to Holy Cross School of Theology in the City of Brookline Massachusetts in Partial Fulfillment of Theology Master (Th. M), Spring 2002.

"Go ye therefore, and teach all nations, baptizing them in the name of the Father, and of the Son, and of the Holy Ghost: Teaching them to observe all things whatsoever I have commanded you: and, lo, I am with you always, even unto the end of the world. Amen."
–MATTHEW 28:19-20

Contents

INTRODUCTION

Purpose and Motivation of This Study

THIS STUDY is an effort that seeks to look into the origins and nature of problems in the history of the Orthodox Church in East Africa and in so doing excite some debate on the history and problems facing the Orthodox Church in East Africa today with an emphasis on nation of Kenya. This study is not intended to provide a chronology of the history of the Orthodox Church in East Africa but rather it looks into the genesis of its present and past historical canonical problems. It is the purpose of this book to lead us, the Orthodox of Africa, into dialogue with each other regarding the state of the Church in East Africa and with a special emphasis on Kenya. This will lead us into self-understanding as well as the discovery of the motive behind our problems.[1] Questions related to the political, cultural, missionary education influences, and African grievances during the colonial era between the years 1919 - 1929, are discussed in *Chapter One*. *Chapter Two* examines the rise of the African Orthodox Church, its journey, aspirations, and its position on ardent issues of reception both by African

---

[1] Zablon Nthamburi, *A History of the Methodist Church in Kenya*, (Nairobi: Uzima Press, 1982), p. 50.

Orthodox of America and Orthodox Patriarchate of Alexandria in relation to canonical questions. Also, the treatment of Anglican orders and sacraments by Alexandria, and the constitution of the African Orthodox Church and its contribution to the present situation in Orthodoxy in Kenya are examined. In *Chapter Three*, a comparison is made between past problems that led to the departure of the African leadership from Protestant denominations, with the African Orthodox Church's current challenges and predicament in relations with the Patriarchate of Alexandria. Finally, in *Chapter Four* the origins of the challenges and problems that face the Orthodox Church in Kenya are discussed with an emphasis on the birth of Archbishopric of Irinoupolis organization. At the end of every segment I try to provide some solutions to the discussed issues and in the end of the book, a skeletal administrative structure, modeled after the GOA, is provided as a viable means of moving us forth in solving our church governance problems.

It has been argued, on one hand, by those who want to show the African initiative in the origins of the Orthodox foundation theory that the founders of the Orthodox Church movement read about the Orthodox Church in the magazines from America, and so decided to follow this true Church.[2] Those who hold to this theory maintain that the desire of African Orthodox founders was purely to find the Old True Orthodox Church and nothing more or less. On the other hand, those proponents of the Greek Orthodox missionary evangelist theory argue that the foundation of the African Orthodox Church was actually an effort of a Greek Orthodox missionary in East Africa.[3] Are these two arguments true? I believe there is more than what these two theories state. While both arguments are not without some truths in them, I propose that there were numerous factors, which led to the foundation of the Orthodox Church in East Africa. Those factors were religious,

---

[2] *The Orthodox Word*, "Orthodox Mission today" July –August 1968. p. 166.
[3] Ibid. p.169.

nationalistic, cultural - traditional, issues of land alienation, and more importantly political issues.[4] They were issues of <u>independence</u> - our fathers wished to free themselves from the religion of and governance by white men.[5] <u>Nationalism</u> - Africans were rising to the new world understanding of themselves and wished to identify themselves more with all that was akin to the African identity, spirit, culture, and re-claim their lost lands, acquire freedom and independence.[6] Even more so, they were issues of <u>Education</u> - education of their children, increment of and subsidizing of Schools, offering of scholarships and labor issues.[7] And the spiritual motives were that although our fathers; Spartas, Obadiah, Matthew, and Arthur George, desired to be free re-ligiously. They sincerely wanted to worship God Almighty and that they wanted to form organizations, which would retain the structure of what, they had known in ecclesiastical organization of their former denominations.[8] This sense of desiring to embrace the oldest Chris-tian tradition and rejecting institutional authorities imbued with overbearing missionary influences, stress the individual and demo-cratic spirit of Protestant foundation in the Orthodox Church. I argue that this Protestant democratic spirit of independence played a big role in educating Africans, about their rights in their quest for free-dom and independence, during the process of the foundation of Orthodox Movements in East Africa. This spirit of independence has been a sources and cause of some of the major problems that have em-battled this Church. Father Spartas and Father Gathuna repeatedly use the words freedom and independence when referring to their move-ments. One desires to be free if they feel they are imprisoned or restrained. One feels the need to move from one social organization or party to another if the party in which one is or finds one's self, does not

---

[4] Jomo Kenyatta, *Kenya: Land of Conflict*, P. 9.
[5] Robert B. Edgerton, *Mau Mau An African Crucible*, p. 19.
[6] Kenyatta Jom, *Kenya: Land of Conflict*, pp. 10–12.
[7] Ibid. pp. 13-14.
[8] Robert B. Edgerton, *Mau Mau An African Crucible*, pp. 20.

fulfill ones needs and desires or if one's principles do not agree with what an organization he is in stands for.

I have chosen this topic with hope that it may shed some light on reasons behind the problems that we face in the Orthodox Church in Kenya today. Apart from fragmental treatment of the history of the Orthodox Church Movements in East Africa by some Protestant historians, there has never been an Orthodox historical study on the problems of the Orthodox Church in East Africa.[9] It is my position that some of the problems which inflicted the Orthodox Church from the beginning and in late nineteen sixties, continue to frustrate its growth, stability, and to contribute to the present Orthodox situation in Kenya, if not in Uganda or Tanzania.[10] In this book, we will then examine and bring into Orthodox perspective the historical origins: canonical, political, cultural social events that have affected and or influenced the organic and spiritual foundation and development of the Orthodox Church in East Africa. These problems will be weighed against the traditional Orthodox positions as found in synodal decrees of the ancient Orthodox Church of the councils and more recent and practical and scholarly experiences of our contemporary historical and canonical Orthodox spheres of different practices. Finally, I will then offer a few suggestions on a possible solution to some of the problems.

It is hoped that this study will open some serious conversation by Orthodox theologians, clergy and laity of Africa, interested in the field of history and canon law, in terms of the facts presented, that is, the themes presented, the content in general, and the setting. For the purpose of this study we will treat the African Orthodox Movements in both Uganda and Kenya as Independent Church Movements, because that is what they were until 1946, when they were officially received into the canonical Orthodox fold, under the wings of the Holy Greek

---

[9] Zablon Nthamburi Ed., *From Church To Mission*, A Handbook of Christianity in East Africa, (Nairobi: Uzima Press 1991), p. iii.
[10] Ibid. pp.16-17.

Orthodox Patriarch ate of Alexandria.[11] The position that the Archdiocese of Kenya holds as the largest Archdiocese in the Patriarch ate of Alexandria, followed by that of Uganda and Tanzania, which formed what was formally the Archdiocese of East Africa, until 1993, calls for its historical canonical study and documentation. What the international community knows about the Orthodox Church of East Africa has come from Protestant writers. First, such writers have very limited knowledge of what they write about and secondly, either there are few treatments here and there of the Orthodox history by a few protestant scholars writing from their fixed perspectives and stand points or some of them writing about their protestant churches, and in passing, throw in a few lines also about the Orthodox Church. This in turn has not been fair reporting on our Church. It is my position that most of what has been written on this subject needs revisiting and are in dire want for correction. A simple example is the name of the founder of the Orthodox Church in Uganda, Spartas. This is a name given to him, according to Sparta himself, by his elementary school teacher, as Sparta, due to his agility in sports, which exemplified the Spartan spirit. He would later add at the end, when he became Orthodox and got to know about the idea of masculine case in Greek language. He got this name way back in his youth and has nothing to do with his future Orthodox mission enterprise. But this name has been so romanticized by many foreign writers in an effort to show, with good intentions, how the Orthodoxy has taken root in this part of the world. Constantine Cavarnos writes:

> He happened to read, when he was young, the history of Greece and was so impressed by it, especially by accounts of the bravery of

---

[11] Ibid. P.17-19.

the Spartan, that he came to love Greece very much, and he gave himself the name Spartas.[12]

There have been, however a few scholars who have treated the Orthodox Church seriously within the realm of independent Churches. Such scholars are: F. B. Welbourn, who in his book East African Rebels: Study of Some Independent Churches, has a substantial treatment of the African Greek Orthodox Church in East Africa from his protestant understanding. David Barret in his book *Schism and Renewal in Africa*, and William B. Anderson has in his book, *The Church in East Africa*, dealt also with The African Karing'a Orthodox Church in Kenya and has given a good treatment of the cultural question of female circumcision. J. A Hughes in his one in two books, East Africa: Kenya, Uganda, and Tanzania, Maryland 1963 and East Africa: The Search for unity Kenya, Tanganyika, Uganda and Zanzibar. Penguin Books 1963, gives a general overview of the cultural and political ramifications in the periods between the declaration of British Protectorate and Independence of East African states.

Besides what we have from our Orthodox sources and my researched conviction, both F. B. Welbourn and William B. Anderson serve as my major reference point on some of the important questions in this paper. I refer to F. B. Welbourn on the questions of the Origin: the founders, and the Constitution of the African Greek Orthodox Church's canonical abnormality, especially on the interviews with the founders, namely Spartas and Father Obadiah Bassajjekitalo, and on reasons why they left the Anglican Church and formed the Orthodox Church. I refer to William B. Andersom and John S. Mbiti on the question of African culture, tradition and politics, which, I believe, are the source of issues leading to the foundation of African Karing'a Orthodox Church in Kenya.

---

[12] Constantine Carvanos, *Meetings with Kontoglo*, (Belmont, Mass: Institute for Byzantine and Modern Greek Studies, 1992) p. 145.

I believe that as we near the end of the first century of our Church life here in East Africa, there is a growing need for the African people, and the like-minded, to explore in a more realistic way the development of this young African Orthodox Church over the years. We especially need to do this kind of work for the sake of our upcoming generations so that they can have a tangible documented study and written history of their Church: to be informed by it, and learn from, admire and to keep. Again, it will serve our later generations well to keep our history as our ancestors managed to do with our nation's oral history.[13] It will enlighten us to glean at what John Kinnamos states in his book about the *"Deeds of John & Manuel Comnenus,"* where he commends about things revealed to us in time, saying,

> Once what had been revealed by time risked being hidden again, but those men who set things down in books as if on the imperishable columns bound them over for continuing life.[14]

---

[13] John S. Mbiti, *African Religion and Philosophy*, Second Edition, (Oxford: Heinmann 1989), pp. 21-23.

[14] John Kinnamos, *Deeds of John & Manuel Comnenus*, Translated by Charles E, Bramuel, (New York: Columbia University press, 1976) p.13-14.

1. The Historical Background – 1900 to 1929

1.1. Historical Background - 1900 to 1929

AN EXAMINATION and assessment in detail of some of the specific underlying issues and factors that contributed towards the foundation of the Orthodox Church in East Africa. The causes and factors leading to the foundation of Orthodox movements in East Africa were similar, in that the region of British Colonial East Africa experienced similar religious and political strife, related to discriminative and racially biased policies that were then prevalent in government and mission enterprises.[15] These similarities are evident in the religious, cultural, and political environment in which these movements were founded. That is why it important to examine the Orthodox Church within the political, social-economic context, because the whole question of the nature of the Orthodox movements in East Africa and Kenya in particular must be viewed within the context of not only religious thought and environment, but also within the whole

---

[15] Bruce Berman, *Control & Crisis in Colonial Kenya*, (London: James Curry, 1990), pp. 121-129.

political, economic, cultural aspects and colonial events of that time.[16] The period, which shaped the young and would be Orthodox leaders tell us about the experiences which they faced and endured, and in which their characters and aspirations were molded, shaped and forever fomented. The stunning events of European missionary, and colonial history: social changes, cultural extermination, religious revolutions as brought and inflicted upon Africa by the west, which tore through colonial African culture like wild fire, formed the religious, political situations, and confused cultural imbalances in which the Orthodox Church was founded. This past of our African culture and subjugation, that touched our lives, is thus very crucial in understanding the Orthodox Church: its aims and objectives as an African social organization emanating from that milieu and founded for propagation of African causes. In this book, I argue that freedom of independence, both religious and political, was the driving force behind the foundation of the Orthodox Church in East Africa. Underlying this major aspect was the educational differences between white missionaries and African adherents especially in regard to cultural understanding of African ontology.[17] Here differences of education and circumcision of females would play a big role but these are among the many issues that go back to the idea of an African freedom, a desire to live and practice what one believed was African without foreign interference.[18] In order for us to appreciate the demands, actions and desires of African people to attain self-rule in religious spheres and political realms, we turn to what was happening in Kenya at the time.

---

[16] David B. Barret, *Schism and Renewal in Africa*, (Nairobi: Oxford University Press, 1966), p. 39.

[17] Ibid. p. 39.

[18] Zablon Nthamburi Ed., *From Church To Mission*, p 17-19.

1.2. The Political Cultural and Influences

What were the political and cultural developments, and crucial events, in between the First and Second World War periods, that influenced the minds of African thinkers of the time, and which moved religious consciousness towards the Orthodox foundation? Harry Thuku, the founder of the first political party in Kenya, Young Kikuyu Central Association, had been arrested, detained and later, on March 14th, 1922, was exiled to Kisimayu[19] Harry Thuku's party was banned and he would remain in jail[20] until 1931. But his popularity and influence shook the whole region of British Colonial Kenya. All the political and religious risings against missionaries and the government trace their origin in that one act of Thuku's arrest and eventual deportation into exile.[21] Later on the risings would be fueled by the missionary effort at eradicating heathen African practice of female circumcision.[22] But seeds of discord had long way been planted over the years in African people's hearts and minds. It was only a matter of time before revolts would set in. As history has learned, what would set the rising off was the last straw, but not the only actual issue of discontent. A keen reading of our African leaders lives and events of their times quickly points to those events that drove them to demand more say in religious missions and in colonial government: a demand for self-rule, more freedom in managing their affairs, and a craving for total independence from missionary and colonial governance.[23] These two,

---

[19] Kismayu is an island in Somalia, on the shoes of Indian Ocean famous for being home to one of the most brutal colonial concentration camps of the time, where many African died in imprisonment

[20] Jomo Kenyatta, *Kenya: Land of Conflict*, (n .p: PANAF Services LTD, n. p), pp. 10 -14.

[21] Gakaara Wanjau, *Agikuyu, Mau Mau Na Wiyathi*, (Nairobi : Thomson Press (1970) LTD, 1971), pp. 36-47.

[22] Zablon Nthamburi Ed., *From Church To Mission*, p.18.

[23] Owen to C.M.S. Secretary, Nairobi, March 23 1923, (C.M.S. Archives Nairobi), B. A. Ogot, A *Place To Feel at Home*, (Nairobi: Oxford University Press,

missionary and colonial governance went hand in hand and Africans understood them to mean or lead to the same. Africans believed that the missionary represented the colonial interest first. This is evidenced by what Canon Owen, who was a trusted champion of African cause in western Kenya, wrote to the governor, when one of the missionaries Dr. Arthur, was requested by the governor to advise on native interests regarding the Indian demands for more rights in the colony. Owen wrote on behalf of missionaries:

> We are of the opinion that your excellency's adviser should be the Hon. the Native Commissioner (who was white). We feel that our educated Natives are very concerned to discover that in question of such importance they are to have no special representation. Any missionary chosen represents European opinion, and has no mandate whatever from the Natives.[24]

The origins of the Orthodox Church must thus be looked at from both religious and political viewpoints because these two both contributed immensely towards its foundation. Early in the 1920's, African leaders in the British colony of East Africa, in most fields: education, and religious especially, were political leaders as well. They were and still are today regarded very highly in political matters and matters pertaining to the whole human society.

1.3. African Mixed Grievances and Challenges

All Independent Church Movements in Africa in particular have their development rooted in the life, both religious and political, of a community. It is through these: religious, political, social economic developments of the time that we can glean at the early foundation of the Orthodox Church in East Africa. There was a litany of African grievances in Kenya by 1920 and above, against settlers and

---

1966), p. 27.

[24] F. B.Welbourn, *The East African Rebels*, (London: SCM Press, 1961), p.128.

missionaries.[25] These problems were reflective of the whole British system of governance in the East African Colony at the time. Economically the Indian Rupee, which was the standard currency, was converted to Shilling and its value depreciated greatly. The majority of African Rupee holders lost their wealth. This conversion affected both Kenya and Uganda. In the process Kenyans and Ugandans lost over 77,000 Sterling Pounds. Welbourn Writes:

> Settlers in Kenya responded to this by reducing wages by one third and forced the government departments to do the same. In 1901 there had been a hut tax of two rupees; and by 1921 both hurt and poll taxes of eight rupees had been imposed and, through a change in financial year, were collected twice within twelve months. ... for the year 1920-21 the estimated revenue from all imports, for Europeans, Indians and natives, was put at 362,250 Sterling Pounds, as compared with an estimated revenue from direct native taxation of 656,070... The non - native tax for the same period was estimated at 21,000 Sterling pounds. The chief Native Commissioner of Kenya in a paper submitted ... Estimated that in 1925 the maximum amount that could be considered to have been spent on services provided exclusively for the benefit of the native population was slightly over one quarter of the taxes paid by them.... in 1929 the government expenditure on African education was 22,000 Sterling Pounds, as opposed to 23,600 on the education of less than 1,000 European Children.[26]

The developing African nationalism then, and struggles for independence in East Africa contributed much towards the foundation of the Orthodox Church movements. The African faith in missionaries and their mission stations was weaning fast. Many African leaders had come to mistrust their missionary brothers and sisters in Christ, since

---

[25] R. Macpherson, *The Presbyterian Church In Kenya*, (Nairobi: Presbyterian Church of East Africa, 1970), pp. 64-69.

[26] F.B. Welbourn, *East African Rebels*, p.122.

many missionaries had completely committed themselves to the policy of compulsory labor, which was very unpopular among Indians and Africans.[27] Even the well-known missionaries who supported the African cause were not spared in this rejection. It had become clear to many that missionaries supported, to some extent, the settler demands that the "local European community should have the sole direction of policy in Kenya. This became more acute when the representatives of the missions attended meetings of the convention of Associations-a settler body."[28] Missionaries also used their higher office to suppress the African claims on land and labor issues. This came on top of the fact that missionaries were landowners as well. Leys, a strong missionary supporter wrote in 1926, there are missionaries whose claim to superior capacities and authorities repel many Indians and Africans.[29] While missionaries clearly fought for more African representation in government, they feared for their own well-being, in case an African would ascent to power.[30] In October 1919 the bishops of Uganda and Mombasa, both Catholics and Protestants together with Dr. J. W. Arthur of the Church of Scotland Mission, as the chairman of the governing board, met to responded urgently to the new government labor circular. Welbourn writes:

(...) by publishing a memorandum in favor of legalized compulsion for labor on government projects instead of the veiled compulsion for all purposes implied by the circular. This memorandum was

[27] Ibid. p.126.
[28] Ibid. p.126.
[29] Ibid. p.126. AIf European, sympathetic to missions, can make allegations of this character, it is certain that educated Africans were feeling more strongly. It is impossible, in a knowledge of the attitude of today, to read in missionary correspondence the constant use of the term "boys" to refer to grown men, without suspecting that it must have been a source of continual irritation to educated Africans as it was explicitly, a few years later, to Reuben Spartas in Buganda.
[30] Zablon Nthamburi Ed., From Church To Mission, pp. 26-28.

later endorsed by alliance of missionary societies. It came under such heavy fire, on one hand from missionary societies and on the other from Christians in the British Isles.[31]

August 1920 saw the introduction of Kaonde system in Kenya, by this order all male Africans of sixteen years and above were required to register and carry a registration paper encased in a metal box and worn around their necks, very symbolic of a dog collar.[32] Failure to observe this ordinance one was liable for 15 Sterling pounds in fines with or without a month's imprisonment.[33] Village headmen, who were government appointees, who failed to deliver able-bodied men for labor, suffered indignities. At the same time Africans were prohibited from growing the rich and profitable Arabica coffee crop then exclusively a white-man's domain.[34]

By now Africans had learned from the minority colonial settlers, who were known to make a lot of noise and demands from the colonial government, and got everything they asked for, that the more organized socially a group was, the more they could protect themselves and safe guard their interests. Africans got to work at it and the more they made noises and demands the more their grievances were heard and solved. One of the missionaries in Nairobi Dr. J. H. Oldham wrote on March 14th, 1922:

> The development of the native peoples in Kenya in one short year and half is simply past thinking. They are almost now able to safeguard themselves against oppression and exploitations. What is much more to be feared is native risings led by young educated Christians and resulting in bloodshed and serious setbacks to their whole life... Propaganda being carried on among all the tribes especially in the semi-educated soil to be found among the young

---

[31]Ibid p.124.

[32] Jomo Kenyatta, *Kenya: Land of Conflict*, pp. 5- 6, 14.

[33] Robert B. Edgerton, *Mau Mau AN African Crucible*, ("n. p", The Free Press, 1989), p. 19.

[34] Ibid.123.

scholars at our schools... Thuku has now got hold of, I should say, the majority of the young Kikuyu Christianity embracing all CMS boys round hooper's neighborhood, our own boys at Tumutumu, but not the older Christians of Canon Leakey's or our lads here. These latter however are called by the others Judases. The movement is anti-European and anti-missionary... We cannot wait now for the royal commission. Things have moved and are moving much to quickly for that. What we are trying to do is to guide this new movement into a right channel and assist them in the righting of their grievances... We are also trying to get them out of the hands of these Indian extremists who are merely using them for their own ends.[35]

It worked for Africans too and soon they were rejecting missionary and colonial directives and, in the process, making both religious and political gains.

By 1923 the British colonial secretary in London had come to a realization that British colonies were not going to be a long term endeavor as it had been earlier envisioned and so it stated in its foreign policy, that in the colonies of Kenya, Uganda and Tanzania, "the African interests were to be treated as paramount, and that while the European interests would be respected, responsible government on the Southern Rhodesian pattern was not to be expected".[36] Though Britain would not honor this policy pledge, under the settler pressure for more lands and rights of governance in Kenya especially,[37] a point of policy had been made and common British folks of good will, who desired to see better treatment of Africans, stuck to it. From here on, the decline of settler pursued interests was set in dramatic mode down the hill, while at the same time the rise of Africans political, social, educational developments was set in slow upward motion. On the

---

[35]F. B. Welbourn, The *East African Rebels*, p.127-8.

[36] Roland Oliver and J.D. Fage, *A short History of Africa*, (Baltimore: Penguin Books, 1962), p. 214. - Refers to Government supported policy of political influence and governance by the settler minority in the colonies.

[37] Jomo Kenyatta, *Kenya: Land of Conflict*, pp. 16-18.

ground in East Africa, the fight for independence was picking up steam. In Kenya for example the Devon shire white paper was published in 1923. This paper explained the British policy in Kenya, and it saw some of the Indian demands met by the government.[38] But Africans were represented by one, white missionary, and one other British official. This period was a period that Africans were refused representation in all spheres of governance. Writing to Mr. Jevanjee in London, one of the staunch supporters of African cause, Mr. Harry Thuku, chairman and founder of the Young Kikuyu Association, wrote: "Real native opinion can only be represented by educated Natives and not missionaries."[39] These words were written almost eighty years ago today, but in our Kenyan Orthodox Church today we are still saying the same to our Cypriot brothers but they do not listen. In 1971 John Gatu, the General Secretary of the Presbyterian Church in East Africa in his speech at mission festival in Milwaukee, Minnesota, pointed out that the continuation of the missionary movement, as constituted at the time was a hindrance to selfhood of the growth of the African Church.[40] It is funny how human kind refuses to read and learn from the signs of the time and past history. Our Greek Patriarchate paternalism of Alexandria has now entered the historical spheres of the protestant dilemma of the Kenya of 1920s. Yet I see no desire by our hierarchy to find some lasting solution to the many problems facing our Church. We hope and pray that it will not be too late for someone to try and right things here in Kenya.

In 1924 the British Colony introduced, indirect rule and local government in Kenya. The name given to it was the Local Native Council (later called African District Council). Though they bore the name Native or African, they were presided over by white men, while the members were officials of the government mostly and some appointed

---

[38] Ibid. p. 11.

[39] F. B. Welbourn, The *East African Rebels*, p. 128.

[40] Zablon Nthamburi, *The African Church at the Crossroads*, A Strategy for Indigenization, (Nairobi: Uzima Press, 1991), P. 71.

African headmen, again who stood for the interest of their masters. The native voice was not given a chance to be heard there[41]

White Kenyan highland was the hot bed of African grievances. Basically the best of African prime land was declared crown land of the British colony and given to willing buyer settlers to develop.[42] By 1923, the now powerful settler community was demanding more and more land and expanding their perimeters and as they did they pushed Africans more and more to the margins of the wild forest. As Settlers gained more land, British colonial government in Kenya created more African home reserves, which were a form of concentration labor camps, to house Africans who had been uprooted from their ancestral homes and lands. So, as Africans lost more and more of their prime land, life became more and more difficult, and very unbearable. Africans were forced to be employed as laborers in white owned farms of what used to be their ancestral land. Africans worked for peanuts, they were paid in cents and given a tin of flour every week called posho. The recruitment into employment was by force and was executed by the local African chiefs by the order of the colonial Native commissioner, who rounded up able-bodied men and sent them off to work. Women and children were also, by order of the Native Commissioner, encouraged to work on white owned farms. If you refused the state would impose unimaginable tax on you called head tax, impossible for a common peasant man to afford.[43]

In 1929 the District Councils were also established here, by British colonial administration but "only Europeans participated in its affairs and decision making, although the majority of the citizens affected by their decisions were Africans"[44] This is the year that Africans announced the official launching of Kikuyu Independent School

---

[41] A. J. Hughes, *East Africa: Kenya, Uganda, and Tanzania*, (Maryland: Penguin books, 1963), p. 98.

[42] Jomo Kenyatta, *Kenya: Land of Conflict*, p.12-14.

[43] Ibid. p. 14.

[44] A. J. Hughes, *East Africa: Kenya Uganda and Tanzania*, p. 98.

Association (KISA) and the African Karing, an Orthodox Church in Kenya. From 1924 to 1944 Kenya experienced a unique and politically very stimulating organ to African political thought, the development of the Legislative Council in the colony. This body had eleven European members sitting on it, one Indian, one Arab and no African. But the production of the Devon shire White Paper 1923 and later 1926-28 spelled the beginning of the end to the legislative council. Hughes put it clearly when he wrote:

> After the first world war, European received their communal roll voting rights and returned their eleven members to the legislative council. The Indians still had just one nominated member and to mark their dissatisfaction with the Devon shire White Paper 1923, they refused to take up the five elected communal seats offered to them...it was not until 1933 that the full complement of Indians elected members sat in the Legislative Council. The ratio of eleven elected European to five Indian members, with one elected Arab continued until after the second world war. Africans interests were supposed to be represented by one, and later two, nominated missionaries and by the officials, but in practice their grievances were more often voiced by the sympathetic Indians.[45]

So then, Africans started to demand total representation in all districts and on all levels of governance.[46] Demands would persist and take all kinds of forms and agitation until the demands were achieved in 1961. The other factor, which helped towards the formation of African associations and in directly therefore, the foundation of the Orthodox Church in East Africa, was the First World War. The First World War gave Africans unprecedented opportunity to get to know the world outside of East Africa and what was happening around the World, which was relevant to the Kenyan situation.[47] This brought

[45] Ibid. p. 99-100.
[46] Gakaara Wanjau, *Agikuyu Mau Mau Na Wiyathi*, pp. 36-39.
[47] Elspeth Huxley & Margery Perham, *Race and Politics in Kenya*, p. 270.

about great change in the African worldview. Huxley and Margery have put it clearly, that the changes taking place in the world at that time were Accelerated by the second world war and all the accumulated pressures released by it.[48] The end of the First World War saw many Africans return home from the war. The majority had lost families and family ties. Many were lame having been crippled from war wounds and came home to nothing. Psychologically, they had been wounded by their traumatic war experiences and were emotionally detached in their majority. Hundreds of thousands of Africans, who served in African Kings Rifle, had died on the battlefield in North Africa, Europe, the Middle East, India, and as far as Burma. War memories would remain with them forever. These war veterans had seen and experienced the strengths and weakness of the white man. The myth about the white man being a great thunder had for them disappeared. They returned home poor and without jobs or with no compensations of any kind by allied victorious forces and found their families evicted from their ancestral land. They realized that they had fought for nothing and had lost their very life possession in the process.[49] Most had gotten some kind of education and experience in the struggle for the Whitman's victory over his enemies. As they returned to East Africa, the Indian Rupee in which they were paid their pennies was losing value and the English Shilling was now taking over as a medium of exchange. The little pay the soldiers received was lost within the exchange rates of Rupee and Shilling. War veterans were frustrated and had many questions that were not answered. They started to join the intellectuals in agitating for more rights: for a return of their lands that had been taken by white men without their consent, for more say in matters of governance, and a return to African practices and traditions. In the process, political temperatures began to rise and tensions set in. The 1920's saw a new development in

---

[48] Ibid. p. 268.
[49] Jomo Kenyatta. *Kenya: Land of Conflict*, pp. 10 - 11.

Above all, cultural issues proved to be the undoing of the missionary efforts in Kenya and in Kikuyu land in particular. There were a number of grievances voiced by Africans over issues of culture and tradition. Which missionaries refused to hear or listen to and address. From the start missionaries had strongly believed that all African cultural practices were heathen and did all they could to civilize Africans. Here the issue of mingling the Gospel with the culture in mission field or(enculturation of the Gospel) arises. Anita suggests that: "One helpful model is (...) where the worshiping community is able to receive and use the import and elements of culture (and thus be localized in a particular context).[50] It must be said that Christ himself was born in a particular culture[51] and he says in Matt. 5:17 that *"I am come not to destroy but to fulfill,"* referring to the Jewish law, culture, and tradition. It is said that St. Innocent of Alaska, who is also called the Enlightener by Russians, showed a remarkable breath of vision on matters of culture and tradition. He was always ready to acknowledge the positive elements acceptable to Christianity that were to be found in the customs of Aleuts and Yakuts of Alaska and their worldview.[52] The Greek fathers, and I have in mind Saints Cyril and Methodios especially but even the whole spirit of the fathers of the East was to uphold the culture and wise capacity of a people in the mission field and to use it to spread the Gospel. The protestant West did the opposite in East Africa. On this cultural issue F. B. Welbourn writes that:

> There were purely ecclesiastical issues in which missionary teaching was strongly opposed to tribal custom. Polygamy and alcohol were generally condemned.... a meeting of the district council at Kiambu on 18th March 1929 recommended legislation against high

---

[50] Stauffer S. Anita, "Worship & Culture", *International Review of Missions*, Vl. 85. 337(1996) p. 182.

[51] Ibid. p. 185.

[52] Kallistos Ware, "The light that Enlightens Everyone: The Knowledge of God Among the Non-Christians According to the Greek Fathers and St. Innocent", *The Greek Orthodox Theological Review*, Vl. 44. 1-4 (1999), p.558.

dowries.... In 1918 the Alliance of missionary societies considered the suppression of "nguiko" (traditional sexual relations between men and women after circumcision and before marriage).... in 1920 the Kikuyu kirk session passed a resolution against what was regarded as an abuse of "Gutugwo", where Christian brides were refusing to enter their husbands' village until they received gifts from every member of the husbands' family.[53]

This last issue if brides being a western influence of a modern Christian wedding. The issue of a gift paid by the bridegroom to his parents- in- laws, before marriage (dowries in western caricature) takes place, was for example completely misunderstood by missionaries to mean bride price and this has stuck to the present. It was not a bride price and indeed the abuse on this practice a rose from this misunderstanding by western missionaries. In its pure African understanding, the so-called bride price is but only a gift, but a very important gift, to the parents of the girl being married.[54] A gift to thank them for raising her up, for allowing the young man to marry her and a significant reminder to the family of the girl that she is important and that she is not gone but lives on in their midst. Her presence in her father's home, though physically absent, is reflected by the gifts of animals that the parents have received from the young man's family.[55]

Missionaries were ignorant of the African feelings and the African discontent.[56] They assumed that they possessed a strong hold on Africans mind, soul and body, through the new crop of educated African men and women that they had brought up in missionary house values.[57] At the same time Africans begun to question the legality of

[53] F. B. Welbourn, The East African Rebels, p.126-27.

[54] Aylward W. F Shorter, African Culture & the Church, (Orbis Books, 1974), p. 127.

[55] John S. Mbiti, African Religion and Philosophy, p. 137, pp .130-141.

[56] Ogot B. A, "The Church OF Christ In Africa", A Place To Feel At Home, pp. 22.

57 Zablon Nthamburi , A History of the Methodist Church in Kenya, (Nairobi:

white-man's land ownership: his sincerity, the authenticity of the white-man's laws, his intentions, and actions.[58] The European racial laws, African land alienation and cultural questions begun to take center stage on the political religious arena of British East Africa. It is in this milieu that educated Africans begun to aspire for political and religious leadership. Mzee Arthur Gathuna wa Gatun'gu, the Orthodox Leader was a teacher who was forced to resign from the missionary school system when teachers refused to sign the opposition to circumcision of females by white missionaries led by the Church of Scotland. He later helped to form Kikuyu Karinga Education Association and become the undisputed Orthodox leaders in Kenya.

It is my conviction that the colonial state in Kenya and the rising political awareness among the educated Kenyans helped to create a situation where Kenyans questioned the validity of colonially associated religious movements and so revolted against the colonially setup institutional structures. The treatment which Africans received from their colonial masters, both in the Churches and in the state offices, was often demeaning and repulsive to Africans. African intellectuals thus sought to use religious movements to foster their hidden political agendas through state and church related activities. After the First World War, in which many Africans took part, suddenly Africans new that the white man was not one powerful nation but rather many and divided, yet loosely related nations, engaged sometimes in fighting each other for political and economic gains.[59] The participation in the war by Africans saw many of them acquire the art of political persuasion through war and the use of force. More Africans had by then achieved high education and saw themselves as intellectuals. The mission church had helped towards the African education; therefore these intellectuals were first and foremost, Christian intellectuals. In

Uzima Press, 191982), pp. 80-84.

58 Kenyatta Jom, *Kenya: Land of Conflict*, p. 12-14.

59 Norman N. Miller, *Kenya: The Quest For Prosperity*, ("n. p." Westview Press, 1984), p. 15.

Tanzania we had Nyerere, Kwame Nkuruma in Ghana, Bonyi in Algeria, Kenyatta in Kenya, Patrick Lumumba in the Congo, and here we include Spartas, Obadiah Basajjakitalo, Arthur gathuna Wa Gatungu and Mzee Matthwe Mulamula and the likes, who were scattered all over Africa fighting for African causes. This new crop of Africans wanted a say in the running of the affairs of their nations.[60] As these new classes of Africans raised their political and religious voices in the colonies, all other sectors of life rose to their support and this included religious cry for more religious as well as political freedom. This freedom assertion included to some extent, the rejection of existing white man's religious influence and formations of structural governance in favor of African leadership and aspiration for what could be identified as African. In general, the new sprouting church movements would keep the skeletal religious structural framework of the missionary church, which could easily be recognized and identified as a church. Thus, for the Orthodox in Kenya we need to give more attention to the Educational and religious conflicts that existed between rising African leadership and the colonial state and religious denominations on the one side. These educational, cultural, and religious problems were heightened and complicated by the rising issues, which we will next examine.

1.4 Missionary Education and its Influence in Religious and Political Struggle

Meanwhile in the period between the First and Second World Wars, Africans went to school and from 1935 onwards, there emerged a new generation of Africans, who had acquired the white man's education.[61] They were smart and appealed to the ears of the African populace, not only from their education point of view but also from the point of view of them being new tools of refraining the white settler

---

[60] Mandela Nelson Rolihlahla, *Long Walk to Freedom*, (Boston: Little, Brown and Company 1994), pp. 364-368.
[61] Roland Oliver and J.D. Fage, *A short History of Africa*, p. 215.

from oppressing their country people. This group of new African thinkers emerged with a capacity to move things, organize political meetings, educational and societal strategies. They quickly claimed their hold on the social ladder and were actively vying for positions and recognition in political spheres and the building of the national social machinery. They were also demanding and appeared poised to take leadership in African states. One thing that missionary education did to Africans was to mold them a new and give them a sense of honor: dignity, responsibility, and respect. But above all, it gave them the idea of freedom and general human rights tenets as presented in western governments policies and the spirit of the gospels that missionaries preached. The settler community was not very happy about this new missionary product. Roland Oliver writes: "some white men in Africa began to speak scornfully of trousered blacks and handfuls of examination-bred students; yet during this second face of the colonial period their appearance was the most important event in African history".[62] This is the period that produced Father Spartas and. Fr. Basajjakitalo of Uganda, Fr. Arthur Gathuna and Fr. Matthew Mulamula of Kenya. It was a period of new thinking and new visions, new political and religious initiatives, new nation weaving and developments. Those people blessed with educational insight, spirit of power, authority, and capacity to move Africa into this new era were missionary educated Christian young men and women of Africa.

The rise of African national movements for political freedom in the 1920's saw the rise in national sentiments and sometime extreme ad vocation for Africanization of all social-economic, and political sectors. It was a time that political movements and their struggles for political freedom were sprouting everywhere in Africa and revolts against the colonial administration setup were common. There was a general understanding among the African populace in Kenya that there was no difference between a missionary and the colonial

---

[62] Ibid. p. 215.

government administrators.[63] It is no wonder then, that during the struggle for political independence in Kenya, for example, the Kikuyu slogan "*Gutiri Mubea na Muthungu*"- (there is no difference between a missionary and a settler)[64] was regularly used to remind Africans that when it came to land question, there was no difference between a white man or colonial masters and missionary priests, they stood for the same thing. The only difference being that they wore different uniforms. The Orthodox Church was thus founded as an African rejection of not only white man's principles, and to some extent, his overbearing religious influence, but also his government over them, politically and religiously. What is striking is the mixture and blending of different strands of thought, culture, political, and religious ideologies that gave birth to a cry for religious and political freedom that eventually saw the birth of the Orthodox Church and political independence of Kenya. On the efforts of the movement for freedom in Kenya, Weigert writes:

> The ideology espoused by dissident members of the Kenyan population who supported the KAU or belonged to a clandestine network organization by KAU (Mau Mau) contained an ambiguous mixture of nationalist and parochial elements. Both the KAU and Mau Mau sought Kenyan independence and land reform. The popular phrase "Land and Freedom," which became associated with the insurgents and those who sought non-violent reform, simplifies what was more complex set of aims and principles[65]

The complexity here must include the fact that the Orthodox religious elements were part of this struggle that begun way back and had seen the birth of the Orthodox Church in mid nineteen twenties. The ideology at work here was national and local, religious and political.

---

[63] Zablon Nthamburi Ed., *From Church To Mission*, pp. 27-28.
[64] F. B. Welbourn, p.111.
[65] Stephen L. Wegert, *Traditional Religions and Guerilla Warfare in Modern Africa*, (D.Colombia: Bureau of Intelligence and Research, Department of State Washington, 1960), P. 24.

The cause was national in the sense that there were issues that touched the social national fiber, such as: achievement of independence, struggle to get our lands back, to free ourselves from both political and religious confinement, by the removal of colonists. This was agreed upon by all forces nationwide involved in the struggle. There were other causes that were not totally national but rather local cultural, such was the case with female circumcision. While the call to reject white teachings on this issue struck a loud accord among groups who did and did not practices this tradition, not all tribes in Kenya circumcise their females. The attack on female circumcision by the missionaries was seen as an attack on the African traditional religious life as a whole and thus it gained its national status as a cause for freedom.[66] It was parochial in the sense not only of locality but also from a religious sense of many different churches as parishes united against a common enemy. All these forces worked together in a combined effort to bring down the colonial forces. The American intelligence sources found this relationship between Mau Mau[67] or freedom fighters and other elements on the ground striking and successful as a political tool to rally the masses for a cause. It states:

> This vanguard emphasized traditional religious and cultural themes and found them useful as a means of mobilizing and motivating a large number of combatants.[68]

---

66 Zablon Nthamburi Ed., *From Church To Mission*, p 18.

67 "Mau Mau," was a code word for the Kenyan Freedom Fighters, in the forest, during the War of Independence form Britain 1948-1956. The movement became so inseparably identified by this code word that it stack as the name for the movement.

68 Ibid. p. 22.

Elekiah Andago Kihali

2. The Rise of the African Orthodox Religious Movements in East Africa and African American Influence

2.1. The Marcus Garvey Factor

THE ORTHODOX CHURCH in East Africa developed from a schismatic movement of a handful, rising young intellectuals in the Anglican, and Scottish missions. In this part of the paper I will endeavor to assess some specific issues encountered during the foundation and reception of East Africa Orthodox Movements into African Orthodox Church of America. There were three movements that sprung up almost simultaneously in East Africa. One was in Uganda led by Reuben Ssebanja Spartas and Obadiah Basajjakitalo and two in Kenya led by Arthur Gathuna in Kiambu, and Mathew Mulamula in Western Kenya respectively. How did the Orthodox Church begin in East Africa? The Orthodox Church came into being about the year 1924 - 1928. By 1929 - 1930 the Church had taken root in both Uganda and Kenya.[69] It begun essentially as a social religious movement but at first it was more prominently associated with educational ideals and

---

[69] F. B. Welbourn, *East African Rebels*, p. 78.

later developed into a religious sect.[70] It would remain a free African Orthodox Independent Church Movement until 1946 when it came under the Greek Orthodox Patriarch ate of Alexandria. There were many events and forces that were now moving the independents and they were powerful and intertwined. But the whole movement was religious as well as political. I am raising these issues to indicate and affirm as discoursed above, that the birth of the Orthodox Church in East Africa was not as a result of one incident or a simple reading of a newspaper or a book about the Orthodox Church and thus founding one. But that it a rose due to myriads of issues and problems in the mission house and field of protestant churches in Africa.[71] Instead of educating Africans for higher levels of office, European missionary desired to train indigenous subordinate staff and wood hewing workers. Often the missionary was found working single-handed in an isolated station.[72] So the major problems and issues facing Africans were related to mission education: they were political, religious, cultural and traditional in nature. I want to stress the fact that these issues all collectively played some kind of role in the events leading to the foundation of the Orthodox Church in East Africa. Welbourn writes that:

> At the time of Thuku's agitation, though without apparent connection, Daudi Maina wa Kiragu formed a small independent church in the village of Gakara, Makindi and Giboro in Fort Hall District. Its members seem to have been drawn from the un-baptized; and its basis was discontent with education provided by missions. Out of the confusion of the 1920s, there emerged two groups with a positive purpose: the Kikuyu Independent Schools Association and the Kikuyu Karing - a Education Association. . . the latter became closely associated with the African Orthodox Church. . . the point

---

[70] Zablon Nthamburi Ed., From Church To Mission, p 17-19.
[71] Zablon Nthamburi Ed., From Church To Mission, p 16.
[72] H. R. A. Philip, *A New Day in Kenya.* "n. p" (World Dominion Press, 1936) p. 20.

which has to be made is that, in all three cases, the explicit basis of separations was disagreement over educational policy: in Fort Hall in 1922 a desire for more(and perhaps better) schools; throughout Kikuyu from 1928 a determination to have education without any ban on female circumcision. If the mission had done nothing else, they had converted men to the magic possibilities of reading and writing; and this they would now have in freedom from missionary control.[73]

Well an impartial reading will reveal to us that these men here mentioned, and their groups were part and parcel of the initial nucleus that would form the Orthodox Church. They were not separate entities in terms of their association and objectives, as Welbourn would have us believe. This disparity a rose from the fact that the group would later split over struggles of the control of schools and each splinter group would try to show that they were the original, and therefore the legitimate fighters for the African cause.

Besides the fight for independence, a major contention for Africans then, was also to keep their religious Practice, in relation to education.[74] They saw religious practice as the center of their lives and regeneration. Welbourn Writes:

In those troubled days we reckoned that religion was necessary to a good and progressive educational system. We found it necessary to have churches where we could pray every day to our creator and Father. We thought of places where our people could train as ministers so that they could teach others about God and his Son Jesus Christ. The need for clergy of our own was obvious in these troubled days, since no one of the other clergy came to our help.[75]

---

[73] F. B.Welbourn, *East African Rebels*, p.144-5.
[74] Zablon Nthamburi Ed., From Church To Mission, p. 19.
[75] Ibid. p. 147.

It is my belief that the choice of the Orthodox Church as the final home for this schismatics came by chance because, they had been shopping around for any church willing to train clergy for them, or post some clergy to serve them, while they tried to settle down, but all was in vain. In the above quoted interview, it reveals that this group was desperate for ministers and could have gone to any lengths to acquire some. Still even with the enormous leadership problem that this young Orthodox independent church movement faced, here and now, they had founded that pure traditional Christianity and purely Africanized both in government, body and spirit. The Orthodox Church had been borne in black Africa, south of the Sahara, in this East African region. This is not to be understood to mean that Christianity was rejected, or that what was founded was fundamentally different from Protestantism, far be it from the truth, they wanted to be Christian in practice and at heart. In fact, apart from the idea of keeping their pure culture intact, they were as protestant as ever before. They sung Africanized Protestant tunes in their churches, used Anglican hymnals and service books. The only thing they rejected was, to do away with their culture, the issue of mistreatment, and enslavement that came via missionary overbearing influence. That is why some Protestant practices have remained "a pain in the neck" for the Orthodox Church in Kenya, to the present, especially as relates to matters of wedding and burial ceremonies, where protestant practices are visibly prominent and a source of agony to those of us, who want to follow the Orthodox Rubrics.

Writing to Marcus Garvey for instructions on how to read the bible and to preach, Spartas says something very important and very revealing about what his true intentions and aims were in founding the Orthodox Church. In his letter to Marcus Garvey, he sends his respects to Mrs. Garvey and tells her that "he had founded the African progressive Association and vowing to go to hell, jail or die for the redemption of Africa"[76] He does not say that he has founded the Orthodox Church, but rather '*African Progressive Association.*' The title of his organization is clearly that of a political association. The title that he gave his new organization tells me that, one; he had not by then, clearly made up his mind about exactly what his relationship with African Orthodox Church in America would be, religious or political. Later on when Spartas wrote to the British Provincial Commissioner in Kampala requesting for the registration of his new organization, he did not mention anything about it being African progressive Association or his intentions to redeem Africa, instead he wrote that his organization "had connections in America, and that it did not interfere with political affairs."[77] Again we see the political diplomacy applied by Spartas in order to survive in a tricky situation. But he was surely leaning towards a political movement. It shows that he had chosen to model his organization on the political wing of Marcus Garvey's organization rather than the religious one. This is not ill intended and there is nothing devious about it. For it is said that: "faith is a slippery thing. It contains the promise of hope and redemption, but also the prospect of bitter disappointment. As such it has much in common with politics, another realm where optimism if often followed by disillusionment"[78] It also shows that this was a man totally committed to the cause of liberation of Africa, religiously or politically, and was willing to die or languish in jail for it. It is also clear here that Spartas was not only a nationalist but was also committed to idea of Pan-Africanism,

---

[76] Ibid. p. 81.
We need to take Spartas very serious on his words because he wished to impress on Mrs. Garvey that he was the right person capable of bring redemption to Africa. Is he referring to religious redemption? The answer is both religious and political.
[77] F. B. Welbourn, *East African Rebels*, p. 81.
[78] Walker Adrian, "A Believer's Rude Reward", *The Boston Globe*, (August 20, 2001)

desiring to see not only the independence of Africa but its political, religious, economical, and cultural unity as well.[79]

The founders of the Orthodox Church in East Africa; Spartas, Bassajakitalo in Uganda and Gathuna and Mulamula in Kenya, did not have in their mind either the Orthodox idea as we know it or even the Marcus Garvey idea of the Orthodox Church in America, under whose organization they modeled their East African Orthodox organizations. Rather they were a class of rising intellectuals of their time, harboring religious and political ideas for independence, and driven by one motive, which was to form a religious and political organization, called a Church, which would be free from missionary influence and governance, free from British colonial dominance, and which would give Africans freedom to govern themselves.[80] It is crucial for us to stress that they wanted to form an organization which would give Africans recognition, respect, honor, and greater religious and political say in matters affecting their African people.[81] They wished to use these organizations as platforms for launching their political agendas and careers. Many Africans had by now learned how to play the political games of the Colonial British in Kenya. They knew that in order to climb up the political ladder, they needed a well-organized and oiled religious, social machinery to do it. Here the religious political organization of African communities before the British occupation needs to be emphasized. Mbiti writes that:

> Where these rulers are found they are not simply political heads: they are the mystical and religious heads, the divine symbols of their people's health and welfare. The individual as such may not

---

[79] Nelson Mandela Rolihlahla, *Long Walk to Freedom*, (Boston: Little, Brown and Company, 1994), pp. 366-368.
[80] Berman Bruce, *Control & Crisis in Colonial Kenya*, (London: James Curry, 1990), pp. 121-128.
[81] Jomo Kenyatta, *Kenya: Land of Conflict*, P. 12.

have outstanding talents or abilities, but their office is link between human rule and spiritual governance.[82]

The social and religious organization of the African kings and their kingdoms: Kingdom of Buganda, Mumia of Western Kenya or the Kikuyu or kamba chieftainship, before the colonial era for example, were a combination of both religious and political offices.[83] The Kabaka was not only a king and ruler of the Baganda but exercised both religious spiritual and political temporal powers. So too did Nabongo of Mumia, Woluyali (His Excellency) Mwami Agoi of Maragoli, and Kikuyu chiefs. Both religious reformers and political activists in East Africa in the early 1920's onwards, and especially in British Colonial Kenya at the time, were striving towards a revival of African traditional beliefs in opposition to western culture introduced by missionaries[84], who were in African eyes, harbingers and imaginary representative of evils, woes, and miseries brought about by settlers and colonists. See K. C.A. statement.[85] An African return to traditional beliefs, and religious practices was therefore, a strong element of the struggle for both political and religious independence.

Reuben Ssebanja Spartas, one of the early protestant products and an ardent African reformer of Uganda, stumbled on some political propagandist magazine of Marcus Garvey's movement for political and religious reform in America.[86] This magazine claimed to foster African emancipation and Spartas was immediately converted to its cause. He immediately got in touch with his friend Obadiah Bassaja Kitalo and began to plan strategies of creating a branch of their own emancipation movement in Uganda. Led by Marcus Garvey's ideas of

---

[82] John S. Mbiti, *African Religion and Philosophy*, (Oxford: Heinemann Educational Publishers, Second Edition, 1989), p. 177.

[83] Jomo Kenyatta, Kenya: Land of Conflict, pp. 7- 8.

[84] Aylward W. F. Shorter, *African Culture & the Church*, pp. 122-128.

[85] Jomo Kenyatta, *Kenya: The Land of Conflict*, p.12.

[86] F. B. Welbourn, *The East African Rebels*, p. 81.

his political and religious movement in America, Africans in East Africa, formed what they believed would drive them to achieve both of their needs, political and religious independence.[87] In order to achieve their goals, they embraced the American style of the African Orthodox Church. When people want freedom, they can go to great lengths to achieve it; or they may do anything to get it. For example, in high lighting the vital role that the Greek Orthodox Church has played on the American scene over the years as an advocate for human and civil rights, Rev. Dr. Constantine N. Dombalis writes in the Orthodox Observer that:

> "people abandon homelands to find it. People cry for it. People fight for it. People die for it... Our beliefs, even in the face of international religious persecution and ethnic destruction have spoken out to governments over the centuries to provide the basic structure of justice."[88]

Spartas, the founder of the Orthodox Church in Uganda, in his letter to Mrs. Marcus Garvey during the early days of his movement vows: "to go to hell, jail, or die for the redemption of Africa."[89] Nelson Madiba Rolihlahla Mandela would say in 1963, in his closing words at his trial, *"I have cherished the idea of a democratic and free society in which all persons live together in harmony and with equal opportunities. It is an idea, which I hope to live for and achieve. But if need be, it is an idea for which I am prepared to die."*[90]

After the First World War there was a lot of resentment and mistrust towards the colonists and missionaries alike. It is agreed that for a while now, Spartas knew that the Anglicanism was not the true faith

---

[87] David Barret B., Schism and Renewal in Africa, p.38-39.
[88] Constantine N. Dombalis, "And the Walls Came Tumbling Down", (*Orthodox Observer* July-August 2001).
[89] F. B. Welbourn, *The East African Rebels*, p. 81.
[90] Nelson Mandela Rolihlahla, *Long Walk to Freedom*, (Boston: Little, Brown and Company 1994), p. 368.

and that he had his own doubts about it and was searching for the true old Church.[91] But from the way he broke from the Anglican Church it is difficult to believe that this is his sole reason for leaving. By the testimony of almost all African Orthodox Church founders we know that things were not going well in the missionary camp and the unhappy campers wanted out. I am led to believe that Spartas was genuinely searching for freedom both spiritual and political. His Anglican bishop read him well when he wrote "*he was a strong individualist, anxious to paddle his own canoe.*"[92] This was before the Second World War, when he had these feelings about Anglican Ordination. But he did not denounce the Anglican Church and leave. After the war Spartas had in 1920 gone back to Kings College Budo to complete his studies. Budo was at that time as Welbourn puts it, "*the highest rung of the educational ladder in East Africa*"[93] We know that Spartas had originally entered Budo on scholarship. This attests to the fact that what we have here was a scholar in the making at the time, whose interests were many and one of them being his desire to be a leading intellectual, educator and a spiritual leader. In those days it was not easy to separate the church from a regular school, as we know it. A missionary served not only as spiritual leaders, but his center served as a school and rounded administration center.[94] From what the African experience was, from the practical experience around them, if you were an educator then you automatically became a missionary. I suspect that this is the kind of leadership Sparta was subconsciously looking for and more. On completion of his studies, he joined the King's African Rifles as a

---

[91] F. B. Welbourn, *The East African Rebels*, p. 77.

[92] Ibid. p. 78. Welbourn adds "and this lends color to the strongly-supported theory that his reason for rejecting ordination into Anglican Church was that it would, first, involve a return to what he regarded as academically inferior climate of Mukono, an Anglican Seminary where he did his junior secondary education."

[93] Ibid. p. 78.

[94] Ibid. p. 173.

private and served as a clerk and an educator at Bombo, where he met his long-term friend, co-founder of the Orthodox Church, and brother in-law-to-be, Basajjakitalo, later to become Fr. Obadiah.[95] But why did Spartas and other leaders break with Anglican missionaries? Reasons are given first by Basajjakitalo, who in 1924 left because, as he put it:

> "had been disturbed by the respect shown to persons by the Angli-can clergy in contrast with the wider charity which he observed among the Roman Catholics; by the origins of the Anglican Church in the divorce proceedings of Henry VIII; and by the absence of the candles, ritual and priestly vestments"[96]

Welbourn adds that had it not been for his wife, Spartas' sister, and Spartas, Basajjakitalo would certainly have joined the Roman Catholic Church.

The behaviors of some missionaries towards their African subjects were not the best at times in East Africa. Missionaries would resort to some measures not different from the brutality of the colonists against their fellow believers.[97] I believe that this unbecoming behavior on the part of some missionaries, not all, contributed much towards the re-sentments that Africans harbored against the traditional protestant Churches and Catholic missions. While we appreciate Basajjakitalo's appreciation of candles and priestly vestments, we observe that at that time he had no practical idea that Orthodox priests wore better vest-ments than those of the Anglican or that in the Orthodox Church lit candles would be readily available. However, we can with confidence feel his desire for more color and glory. But the major reason that led him to depart from the Anglican Church was the treatment question, by the Anglican clergy. As for the divorce proceedings of King Henry VIII of England, leading to the foundation of the Anglican Church, I

---

[95] Ibid. p. 78.

[96] Ibid. p. 78. See also - Robert B. Edgerton. *Mau Mau An African Crucible*, p.20.

[97] B. A. Ogot, *A Place To Feel At Home*, Church Of Christ In Africa: "Church in Crisis", pp. 40-44

totally agree that if Basajjakitalo cared deeply about his faith, this was a serious problem. But again, he did not have a better faith of the Orthodox Church at his disposal, at the time, in order to compare the two. Though he may have read some historical books and certainly new about the existence of the Orthodox Church. There is no evidence, however, to suggest that he knew what the Orthodox believed or how their kings made decisions concerning matters of divorce and faith, in order to compare the two and make a final decision. What we can make of this is that Basajjakitalo was reading about other faiths because he was not satisfied in the Anglican faith and that he wanted out. Why? Because missionaries used to call African men, boys, and in practice treated them as such. Testifying about the African state in S. Africa in 1963, Nelson Mandela states that: *"the lack of human dignity experienced by Africans is a direct result of the policy of white supremacy. White supremacy implies black inferiority. Menial tasks in South Africa are invariably performed by Africans."*[98] Some missionaries were harsh, racist, and inconsiderate sometimes towards their African subjects and greatly lacking in the love and mercies of God, dispensing of charity in practice. Lack of charity in a church could and did eschew the idea of the love of God, care, and understanding that missionaries preached.

It seems that while serving in King's African Rifles, Spartas realized that he was not cut for being a subordinate staff in the field, which he believed himself to be the master: the intellectual, spiritual, and political field. At that time Spartas was serving as an orderly under the supervision of Lieutenant Twining, later to become the governor of Tanganyika British Protectorate.[99] Spartas weighed his capabilities against his immediate superiors both in the Anglican Church and the British Protectorate in Uganda and saw himself the better of his superiors. This is seen in the way he systematically and strategically, carefully planned, together with Basajjakitalo, to resign in 1925, from

---

[98] Nelson Mandela Rolihlahla, *Long Walk to Freedom*, (Boston: Little, Brown and Company 1994), p. 367.
[99] F. B. Welbourn, *The East African Rebels*, p. 78.

a paid government clerical service, which was considered very lucrative at the time, and to form their own school, where they could be their own masters. About this time Welbourn has it that, "Spartas had seen the Negro World (magazine) and was investigating as fully as possible the Garvey Movement and African Orthodox Church in America"[100]

We need to state up-front, that the Marcus Garvey Movement did not come across to Africa via its paper in a form of a church newsletter to inform Africans of this great traditional Orthodox Church that was ready to receive them. It was a political propagandist paper trying to reach a wider African readership and to recruit them into their political organization and agenda. Its aims were to arouse negative African sentiments and resentment against White Americans first, who were then oppressing blacks allover, and in turn arouse Africans against their colonizers in agitation for greater African unity in social, economic, and political realms. It is my conviction that the Marcus Garvey movement influenced Spartas towards African emancipation. He was following the Marcus Garvey's ideas as preached in the emancipation politics and African Orthodox movement in America. Spartas saw freedom, as a stepping-stone towards a raise in rank of African religious leadership, political leadership and unity, economic success, and freedom of independence in their own countries. Welbourn states *"The African Orthodox Church, which sprung from the Garvey Movement, offered emancipation and high ecclesiastical rank denied to Negroes by Protestant Episcopal Church of America."* [101] Spartas in like thought stated that he was ready to liberate Africa.[102] Liberation is always liberation of freedom no matter if we want to advance the theory that Sparta was referring to a spiritual salvation or actually to a social and political salvation. James H. Cones in his book *"God of the Oppressed"* states that:

---

[100]Ibid. p. 79

[101] Ibid. p. 79.

[102] See Spartas to Marcus Garvey quoted above.

There is no liberation independent of the struggle for freedom in history. History is the immanent character of liberation; it is the project of freedom. The immanence of liberation is visible whenever the emancipation of the people from the chains of slavery takes place in history. There is no liberation without transformation that is without the struggle for freedom in this world. There is no liberation without the commitment of revolutionary action against injustice, slavery, and oppression. Liberation then is not merely a thought in my head; it is the sociohistorical movement of people from oppression to freedom [103]

Spartas and his fellow Africans were under colonial oppression and experiencing similar predicaments here in East Africa to that of black Americans at the time.

Who was Marcus Garvey that he would influence Spartas' religious life and political quest so much? Now if we understand Marcus Garvey and his agenda, I believe we will be close to understanding Spartas and his quest for religious and political freedom in East Africa. It was only after studying Garvey's movement very carefully that, Spartas was convinced that here laid the solution to African problems. Marcus Garvey, was:

A Jamaican Negro, who in 1914 founded the Universal Negro Improvement Association, described himself as the 'provisional president of Africa, created African orders of nobility, established an African Orthodox Church, published the Negro World, and organized international conventions for Africans, and non-African Negroes-was successful in spreading the idea of independent African churches as an instrument of African liberation. The impact of Garveyism' can be traced in British and French West Africa and the Cameroons, as well as in South Africa, particularly during the

---

[103]James H. Cones, *God of the Oppressed*, (New York: The Seabury press, 1975), p.152.

period of unrest and revolt that immediately followed the First World War"[104]

These, in a nutshell are the principles guiding the Marcus Garvey Movement and his associates: Archbishop and Patriarch of all the Orthodox George Alexander Macguire, and Archbishop Daniel William Alexander of South Africa. To these principles Spartas of Uganda, Arthur Gathuna, and many Africans of their time prescribed, embrace and religiously followed.

What is it that drew Spartas to the ideals and principles of Marcus Garvey? What fascinated Spartas, and therefore, the African leadership about Macus Garvey and his Orthodox movement in America was not only a faith of a historical church, whose doctrines and tradition they wished to espouse. There was more, for Garvey did not have doctrines, his was African Religion gone political. Of cause Spartas and his comrades wanted a true and pure Orthodox Faith. But more importantly it was rather, what Marcus Garvey stood for and, what the African Orthodox Church in America seemed, in ideal, to promise to offer to the would-be African partners and members in the struggle, that pulled Spartas to ideals of Garvey. The Orthodox Church in America gave them hope in the future of Africa. Hope that it was possible to defeat the colonizing oppressor of the west and his culture. Hope that together united blacks of all walks of life could rise against their common enemy, the white oppressors, and defeat him. The African leadership's motive and desire to be Orthodox was not driven by a great longing to be part of a magnificent spiritual wisdom that surpassed that of the Anglican and or Scottish missionary denominations, that they knew. If their desire was otherwise than what I state here, then the evidence pointing to this has been shrouded in the untraceable oblivion of the past. Yes, we have agreed that there was a true desire to find the true Old Christian Church, the Orthodox Church, but this is only a part of the equation not the whole of it. It was

---

[104]F. B. Welbourn, *The East African Rebels*, p. 79.

not the clarity and purity of the Orthodox faith as manifested in its belief, and that it was founded by Jesus Christ and the Apostles that steered Africans forth, but rather, they were steered by its projected prospect of freedom as proclaimed by Marcus Gavery's ideals. It was not entirely the force and power of realization of the Orthodox truth, neither was it its continuing history from the long history of the ancient Church fathers, that pulled our founding fathers to Orthodoxy, but rather it was a desire for equality of all races, that propelled them into the faith of the Fathers. In the historical achieves of the founders of the Orthodox movement in America: Macus Garvey, George Alexander Mcguire, and Daniel William Alexander in South Africa, there is no clear explication of what one can theologically call an Orthodox a faith. Yes George Alexander Mcguire claims some ordination from some questionable canonical prelate in Europe but that is it.[105] Beside the fact that George A. Mcguire is a product of political and religious ambitions of Marcus Garvey and therefore secondhand product to the actual principle driving his movement itself, does he have an Orthodox creed, or a declaration of elements of Orthodox faith? The answer is no! The creed that Bishop G. A. Mcguire followed was a protestant one. When Archbishop Daniel William Alexander arrived in Uganda in 1931 to ordain our first African priests, his service book was the Anglican service book![106] If there was some kind of profession of faith different from the one Africans already knew, we could then point to it and say yes, this is what the Africans read in the papers and were thus convinced? Of course, there is nothing like that. The profession of faith that is to be found in the Anglican service book is that typical western style creed with the Holy Spirit proceeding from both the Father and

---

[105] F. B. Welbourn, p. 79.

[106] Ibid. pp. 86 - 89. Before his arrival to Uganda Archbishop A. William wrote Sparatas alerting him of the list of the things needs at ordination: Tunicle, Alb, Chasuble, Chalice, Paten. I will bring the Bible with me, he says, but does not mention a Divine Liturgy book because he did not have one.

the Son (*"filioque"*).[107] Is this an Orthodox faith? Or better yet, was this a new teaching that would excite Spartas or Basajjakitalo so much that they would want to change their faith considering that they both had been Anglicans since they were toddlers? No! They both were very familiar with it. The only thing that struck the Africans about this American movement was the idea of equality expressed in these three words: African Church, Unity, and Freedom - both religious and political. Theirs was simply a search for a church, which did not discriminate, enslave, and colonize them. A church, that would grantee principles of equality and freedom to Africans. A church which did not have a connection with colonial masters, and which was not going to impose a new and foreign culture upon them. Because they were tired of what they had by now recognized as western cultural, religious and political cynical paternalism.[108] In like manner Mandela stated at his trial in 1963 that: *"Africans want a just share in the whole of South Africa, they want security and stake in society. Above all we want equal political rights, because without them our disability will be permanent."* [109]

When the African leadership, namely Spartas and Bassajakitalo, read about the Orthodox Church from the view of Macus Garvey and his African representative, they were struck by moving practical ideals for African struggles such as removal of the oppressor: independence, African self-reliance, African unity, and total disregard for the faith of the white man. Africans wanted to have what the settlers had. Huxley has put it thus; it was the desire for equality that seems to move individual, classes and nations with an energy never shown before in

---

[107] See The Great Synod of Constantinople 1472- 1475,which denounced the council of Ferrara – Florence on the Union and Doctrine of Filioque.
[108] F.B. Welbourn, *Religion and Politics in Uganda*, East African Publishing House 1965, p. 11.
[109] Nelson Mandela Rolihlahla, *Long Walk to Freedom*, (Boston: Little, Brown and Company 1994), p. 368

history.[110] The other reason for Africans quick acceptance of the Orthodox Faith is that, African leaders were desperate to get out of Protestant churches, and get started in a new home. They wanted to be somewhere, and fast so, that they could *be fulfilled in their own land and continue to exercise their religious rites.*[111] Spartas had correspondence even with the Anglican Bishop whom he had broken away from and begged him to send priests to serve his new community on loan until, when they would get their own priests.[112]

In founding the Orthodox Church, Africans wanted to reconstruct their fallen identity and reclaim their lost religious, cultural, and political values during colonization by proclaiming their Church independence. That African leaders wanted something different from that of western European culture, is evident in the name that our Father in Kenya Arthur Gathuna, gave to his new-found organization. He did not just find an Orthodox Church but rather Orthodox Karing, African purity. This word *"Purity"* is the most important key to our question here. The name of the new found organization was African 'Karin'ga' Orthodox Church the key is in the word Karin'ga, which is a Kikuyu word meaning pure, the purity of the 'Agikuyu people and tradition,' Agikuyu way of life, Akikuyu culture.[113] It is also easy to argue that our fathers used it to mean the purity of the Orthodox Faith. Indeed, today this word is well within the right vocabulary of the holy Orthodox Faith. Did they mean the purity of Orthodox faith from the beginning? The answer is no. The Orthodox Parish of St. Pathenios Waithaka, which I served from my ordination to the priesthood until my coming to the state in June 2001, is home to some very unique individuals, who were young men serving as warriors or messengers of

---

[110] Elspeth Huxley and Margery Perham, *Race and Politics in Kenya*, (London: Faber & Faber Ltd Mcmxlv), p. 268.

[111] Nelson Mandela Rolihlahla, *Long Walk to Freedom*, (Boston: Little, Brown and Company 1994), p. 366.

[112] F. B. Welbourn, East African Rebels, p. 86-87.

[113] Wanjau Gakaara, *Agikuyu, Mau Mau Na Wiyathi*, p. 52.

freedom fighters movement, or combat guerilla fighters during the Mau Mau struggles or whose parents were officials in the struggle. I believe their statements are very accurate and reliable. I have discussed this issue with Mzee Daniel Mukuria and Mzee Timothy, and these Wazee's - Elders, tell me that the word *Karing* referred to the pure undiluted African Kikuyu livelihood, culture, tradition, and spirit. In Mr. Mukuria's recent letter to me he emphasizes the point of freedom that the founding fathers fought very hard for. He writes:

> We are looking up to you, and those who will follow after you. Our fathers were praying and working had to educate their children so that they could deliberate (sic) (he wants to mean liberate) themselves from slavery. They have passed away from this world but we shall not rest until the time we shall have cut all links of chains off.[114]

The word *Karing* meant African purity as a whole, and as opposed to the diluted western influences which were now cropping up in their midst and taking central stage in the African homes through the teachings of missionaries.[115] Folklore music were formulated, sang and danced to, in the now popular and familiar war like tunes of Muthirigu,[116] in order to encourage Africans to adhere to the purity of Agikuyu and at the same ridiculing, attacking, and castigating the looseness of western life style and culture. It worked to the advantage of freedom fighters. Many young men rallied behind this movement as it sought to uplift the traditions that beheld men to be heads of homes and not boys. The cultural political ramification of this name, Orthodox Karing, is obvious. The new Orthodox Church stood for the

---

[114] Daniel Mukuria to Father Anastasios Kihali, 3rd Sept. 2001. - One of the leading elders of St. Pathenios Orthodox Church in Waithaka, Nairobi.

[115] Wanjau Gakaara, *Agikuyu, Mau Mau Na Wiyathi*. p. 52. -The Muthirigu dancers sung that they were the purity of Agikuyu and they could not change their religion - My translation.

116 Wanjau Gakaara, *Agikuyu, Mau Mau Na Wiyathi*, P. 53.

defense of the African culture, identity and tradition against the westernization of Africa culture by European missionaries. This idea of purity and return to African tradition had a very powerful appeal to Kenyan people both from a political and religious point of view. The response from the local populace was enormous. People flocked to the Orthodox Church in huge numbers. The church registry for new members hit very high margins than never before. The European missionary enterprises were on the other hand losing their flocks' en mass.[117]

African elders break from the mission churches was not therefore, so much a doctrinal issue as it were a quest for traditional cultural roots, African identity, and freedom from the influences of the missionary. Certainly, three things drove Spartas: a search for religious truth, political freedom and explicit nationalism, leaning towards pan Africanism. The line between religious and political ambitions driving the break from the mission churches was not always very clear. Oliver Roland says that some of the opposition to the missionary enterprise and colonial set up:

> (...) were not overtly political. Thus in eastern, central, and southern Africa, where Christian missions often preceded European administration, and where the development of European settlement could lead to severe maladjustments in African society, African opposition sometimes found expression in *Ethiopianism* - the formation of separate and specifically Negro Christian Churches in which beliefs and practices learnt from the mission were often colored to suit local ways. The members of such churches might on occasion break out into blind revolt against the European administrators and settlers, who generally regarded them with suspicion and hostility.[118]

---

[117] F. B. Welbourn, The *East African Rebels*, p.127-8.
[118] Roland Oliver and J.D. Fage. *A short History of Africa*, p. 239.

European administration was very hostile to descending views at the time of the foundation of the African Orthodox Church. That Africans were tired of the European dominance, lack of respect for African clergy and people in general, is expressed in their desired for self-governance and also to have dignity in one's own land and country. To become a priest was very difficult though the Africans did the actual work of pastoral care, catechism leading to baptisms of initiates.[119] Spiritually therefore, Africans were malnourished. They could not feed their own flocks in the best way they knew how because they could not be let to do so. They were asked many times than not to reject their traditional beliefs and values.[120] This trend tented to break the African cultural backbone but gave no alternative culture for Africans to hold on to and keep the African family unit together. The Gospel, which was preached was not rich enough or was a divided loose amalgamation of western thoughts and cultures, which did not fit in the African environment. It left a big vacuum in the African psychology and confused his culture so much that they started to resent having joined the missionary churches in the first place. It was inconceivable for example for the Scottish mission to think in the 1920's that Africans were going to give up circumcision of females. Over seventy years later, today, this practice is still very strong in Kenya and Churches and governments are still strongly opposed to it.

2.2. Reception by African Orthodox Church of America, Growth, and Challenge, 1928-1932.

We need to appreciate the patience with which Sparta waited to be received into the African Orthodox Church of Marcus Garvey. He had made the first contact in 1924 and in 1925 he wrote Marcus Garvey[121] requesting for instructions on how to read the Bible and how to preach

---

[119] B. A. Ogot, "The Church OF Christ In Africa". *A Place To Feel At Home.* pp. 21- 24.
[120] Wanjau Gakaara, *Agikuyu Mau Mau Na Wiyathi*, pp. 51-55.
[121] Ibid. p. 81.

but there would be no reply until 1928. In this letter, it seems that he presumed that he had already been accepted as a member. The news that Spartas received from Garvey, almost three years later were more than good. He told him of the consecration of an African Bishop in South Africa and asked him to get in touch with him. Garvey also asked him if he was still interested.[122] Here we feel the desire, commitment, and ambition of Spartas to be a leader. Immediately on hearing from Marcus Garvey, he replied:

> I am still hundred percent for the purpose. I am prepared to go from field to field throughout Africa. I wish I were already made an active member of AOC... Encourage me and empower me whether I may start the work... I wish I were just like that active son of South Africa who was made primate and Archbishop of South Africa.[123]

In the same year 1928, having been put through by Marcus Garvey, Archbishop Daniel William Alexander of South Africa, appointed Spartas as a lay reader under his supervision.[124] This appointment by letter was purely protestant in nature. There is nothing Orthodox about it. No *"cherothesia"* ordination was done or prayers said. I am raising this as a canonical issue pointing to the very humble abnormality in the Orthodox Church roots in East Africa. But as un-canonical as it is, this letter of appointment gave Spartas what he wanted, recognition, a key of belonging to an international Orthodox Church and a permission to begin work in earnest. Spartas announced his break with the Anglican Church and the formation of a new Church,[125] on the 6th of January 1929.

The title of the new Church was *The African Orthodox Church* - an African Church governed by Africans for Africans. A church, established for all right-thinking Africans, men who wished to be free in their own

---

[122] Ibid. p. 81.

[123] Ibid. p. 81.

[124] Ibid. p. 81.

[125] Ibid. p. 81

house, not always being thought of, as boys.[126] This title is the center of all the present problems of the Orthodox Church in East Africa both past and present. First, we have an organization, which sprouted from a political milieu mixed with uncanonical religious beliefs by uncanonical leadership. This movement would start to grow in a hot political and religious climate but essentially exhibiting a sense of political freedom as espoused by the western political organizations, represented by the African Orthodox Church of Marcus Garvey in America. Secondly, it professed to be Independent. The problem for East African Orthodox, after joining the Patriarchate of Alexandria, was, and still is that in the minds of Africans, that the idea of independence was a given. They believed it, and it is still there today. It was never taken away. This great misunderstanding on the part Africans on one hand and on the part of Greek missionaries on the other is due to a refusal by missionaries over the years to listen to African grievances and the assumption that the missionary knows what the problem is and that he has the solution to everything. Only Africans will solve this problem given the right climate and a good listening ear. Yes, Spartas accepted to join Alexandria but did so with his independent movement intact both in belief, structure, and constitution, which stated that his movement was an independent one. He was never told, look it is over, and you are now under the immediate supervision of the Bishop of East Africa, under the patriarch of Alexandria. This was a very dear canonical oversight, in my view, on the part of Alexandria.

African Orthodox Church founders in East Africa were essentially schematics from the Anglican Church and the Scottish missions. At the time Spartas had communications through correspondence with both the Anglican leadership in Uganda and in London, and later had similar correspondence with Alexandrian Orthodox leadership.[127] So every side knew what was going on in East Africa, at least in Uganda.

---

[126] Ibid. p. 81.
[127] Ibid. p. 83.

It is agreed that neither Spartas nor his friend Basajjakitalo were ordained ministers at the time of the foundation of the Orthodox Church. They were laymen so the question of ordination is not that strong an objection at first but is complicated by the fact that they would, later be ordained by Bishop William Alexander, yet another, upshot of schematics.[128] The Marcus Garvey movement in America sprung from the Anglican Church of America popularly referred to in America as Episcopalians.[129] This brings us round about and to point zero where we began with Anglican orders. We need to a certain the validity of the bishop who bestowed blessings of ordination by the laying on of hands on East Africa's first Orthodox clergy. Was Bishop Alexander of South Africa's ordinations canonical? Bishop Alexander, a native of South Africa, was himself consecrated by Archbishop George Alexander Macguire, a member of the Marcus Garvey movement, who was not only primate of the African Orthodox Church in America but the Patriarch, Alexander of the African Orthodox Church of the World, and was himself consecrated by Joseph Rene Villatte.[130] At this point, we agree that we are dealing essentially with Episcopalian Schematics who have received their Episcopal orders from Joseph Rene Villatte. And just who was this man Villatte? For the answer to this question we turn to Wellborn, who states that:

> Since validity of these orders was a question of moment of not only to the Anglican Church in Uganda, whose territory had been invaded, but later both the Church of Kenya and Greek Orthodox in Alexandria, it is necessary to summarize Brandreths account Villatte (Episcopi Vagentes, pp.31-34) Joseph Rene Villatte was a Parisian who early emigrated to the United States of America and trained for Roman Catholic priesthood. After numerous changes of the religious allegiance he received in 1885 deacon's and priest's orders from an old Catholic bishop in Switzerland, took oaths of

---

[128] Ibid. p. 79-80.
[129] Ibid. p.79.
[130] Ibid. p.79.

canonical obedience to the Episcopal bishop of Fondu Lac and worked among Belgians Old Catholics in Wisconsin. After several attempts to achieve Episcopal consecration, 1892 he repudiated the jurisdiction of his bishop and was excommunicated. He declared himself elected as Old Catholic Bishop in America. On 29th May 1892 he was consecrated bishop by archbishop Alvaeres of the Independent Catholic Church of Ceylon and two other bishops. Alvaers himself was a dissident Roman Catholic who on the authority of the Jacobite Patriarch Ignatius Peter II of Antioch, had been consecrated in 1889 by the Jacobite bishop of Kottayam in Malabar and put in charge of schismatic Latins Catholics in the Ceylon. After ordination Villatte proceeded on his sole authority and without assistance of other bishops to consecrate others in various parts of the world[131]

It is clear from an Orthodox canonical Perspective that we are dealing here essentially, with heretical orders. If we look at the last sentence there that he proceeded on his sole authority and without assistance to consecrate others in various parts of the world, we get the idea that such ordinations in Orthodox communion are invalid as if they did not take place.[132] In our Orthodox experience today both in the ecumenical Patriarchate and Alexandria, there are two ways followed when electing a bishop. Either:

He is elected by the competent Episcopal synod and ratified by the secular authority (as is the case in Ecumenical Patriarch ate) or he is elected by an assembly in which the hierarchy and representatives from among the laity take part as is the case in Cyprus[133]

Also, Alexandria uses the same practice - in theory.

---

[131] Ibid. p. 80.

[132] The Very Rev. Jeronimos Cotsonis. "The Validity Of The Anglican Orders According To Canon Law Of The Orthodox Church" Greek Orthodox Theological Review 4 (1958). pp. 44 – 47.

[133] Professor Lewis J. Patsavos. Manual for the course in Orthodox Canon Law. Mass. 1975. p. 91.

It is difficult to imagine that people who had been raised in the faith and educated, and made what they were by the good fortunes of the Western ideals of religion and civilization, could turn around and reject it. But for Spartas and his counterpart in Kenya, it was a rejection of paternalism not western education or lifestyle or to some extent, even religion. This newfound faith was the alternative and long a waited for religious movement founded by Africans. They did not see it as rejecting of their mother Church but rather they saw themselves as seeking the fullness of their human African identity, religious dignity and honor, which their mother Churches had denied them. The church shall be called the *African Karin'ga Orthodox Church*, in the words of Father Arthur Gathuna, and Spartas stated: A church established for all right-thinking Africans, men who wish to be free in their own house, not always being thought of as boys[134] This was going to be a church of Africans, ruled by Africans, for African people. A church where men would be recognized as men and not little boys, but as the colonial masters preferred to call African men. This phenomena of revolt and rejection of mission Church and culture, which espoused, what appeared to Africans to be colonialism, was not akin to East Africa only, but reflected a wider feelings a cross colonial territories of Africa both French and British alike.[135] Many African individuals and leaders collectively as isolated nations had tried different methods to get rid of white colonizers, but failed.

A class of young and educated Africans then, in the periods after the First World War, began to experiment with the ideas of forming social organizations, once they learned from the settler political cliché that social organization was key to getting political unity, agitation for independence, and for getting hearing by their colonizers.[136] They undertook to form social associations, which were politically inclined, if

---

[134] Ibid. p. 81.

[135] Author Unknown, *The Church in Rwanda*, Nairobi: African Publishing Company 1977), pp. 152-55.

[136] Ibid. p. 152.

not full flagged political parties.[137] Spartas was one of the earliest to form such an organization. In early 1920s he founded, *The African progressive Association* followed by the *Christian Army for Salvation of Africa* and finally - a more lasting endeavor - *The African Greek Orthodox Church*[138] Did our church elders then want to be Orthodox? Yes, but initially, only as far as it would be the African wing of Marcus Garvey's African Movement for religious freedom and political independence in America, and now on the African soil fighting hand in hand with his African brothers against white dominance. East African political and religious thought among the African people.

In Kenya, both the *Kikuyu Karinga Education Association* (KKEA) and *Kikuyu Independent Schools Association* (KISA) began as one movement and only separated later due to regional and inter-personality clashes. KISA was from the North, Mount Kenya region of Central Province, and KKEA was from the South in Kiambu and what is now Nairobi Province. Leaders from the north always suspected and mistrusted the intentions of the southerners. The published policy statement of KISA is said to be the only statement available and that KKEA did not have a policy statement.[139] This is not true because the statement of KISA was issued 1929 at the time that the two were still together as one organization and that is why we have only one statement. If need be let it be told that in 1935 Archbishop Daniel William Alexander Ordained the, would be first two priests of the Independent Pentecostal Church, within the Orthodox Church.[140] After Uganda Archbishop Williams arrived in Kenya at the end of 1934 and begun ordinations in 1935. He Ordained Gathuna and two others from the north as Orthodox Priests and they did function as such for a while before the split of the whole

---

[137] Ibid. p. 152.

[138] F. B. Welbourn, *African Religion & Politics in Uganda*, (Nairobi: East African Publishing House, 1995), p. 11.

[139] F. B. Welbourn, p. 145.

[140] D. E. Wentink, The Orthodox Church in East Africa, The Ecumenical Review vol. 20, WCC, January –December (1968) P.35

independent Schools organization into two Organizations. In any case the so called KISA policy statement gives the true picture of the issues of discontent that were motivating our church fathers at the time and the reasons behind the formation of the organization which would give birth to the Orthodox Church. F.B. Welbourn states that:

> KISA was established, according to its published statement, in 1929, the federal creation of independent school committees in the various districts of central province. Its objects were-to further the interest of the Kikuyu and its members and to safe guard the homogeneity of such interest relating to their spiritual economic, social and educational upliftment[141]

Here rests the genesis of the spirit of the Orthodox Church in Kenya. The same can be said of Uganda with accuracy, given Spartas clearly pronounced and stated constitution of the African Orthodox Church. All the differences that we have experienced in the Orthodox Church in the past and present, with missionaries, emanated and still do today, in my view, from lack of understanding of the spirit, interest, and principles that guided our founding fathers and therefore, the African leaders (behind the scenes) of our Church today in Kenya. This spirit is completely lacking in missionary mind set. I want to suggest that this KISA statement could be used as a bridge between local Orthodox natives and missionaries as some sort of a point of convergence in our dialogue with the missionary enterprise in trying to solve our problems in Kenya today.

The Independent movement was now two-fold, in that the power of the movement lay in establishment of schools and religious worship centers. At every point and place that a school was started, religious observance went hand in hand with it. Soon there were schools operating as churches on Sundays and during weekdays they would house pupils as schools. In all counts both church and school organization were initiated at the grass root level. Parents did donate land on which

---

[141] F. B. Wellborn, p.145.

to erect the buildings, poles, rails, and roofing materials. Schools stationary, stipends or wages for their teachers were also the responsibility of parents. Men went to erect school structures while women fetched water for making mud for smearing the same mud structures. It was a spirited teamwork. The result of this effort was the birth of *The African Karinga Orthodox Church*, hundreds of Schools, and of two organizations Kikuyu Karinga African Schools Association in central, Nairobi and Kiambu districts and Kikuyu Independent Schools Association in Nyeri and Embu, mostly. These two organizations would work together for a while as two wings of the African Karinga Orthodox Church but splitting radically in two separate movements with two different religious agendas. Kikuyu Karinga African Schools Association would remain part of the Orthodox Church and a strong educational cum political wing of the church. It was here through this organization that the Orthodox voiced their grievances both social and political.

This is how the Orthodox Church was founded in Kenya. It came as a revolt against the oppression of Africans by missionary enterprises. The African members of mission churches who refused to sign the declaration against female circumcision had nowhere to worship. The only option for them was to form what they thought was close to what was practiced in their former churches. The choice of the Orthodox Church seems to have come to them by chance on learning that the Orthodox Church in America was led by Africans and had African interest at heart.

It will suffice here to state that both Spartas and Arthur Gathuna were educators and politicians in their own rights. Sparta tried his hand in politics in Uganda by forming his own political party, the Bataka Progressive Party, but it did not go far. His counterpart in Kenya, Arthur Gathuna, was on the other hand a very successful politician who served in the Nairobi City Council as an elected councilor for many years. The General Secretary of the African Karin'ga Orthodox Church in Kenya for many years, Fr. Elefetherios Ndwaru, now retired, served also as a councilor in Nairobi City Council for many years. The treasurer of the Orthodox Church in Kenya in the seventies and eighties, Fr. John Ngugi N'gethe was and is still today a Councilor in Nairobi City. Orthodox elders were also fine politicians who agitated for political freedom of Kenya. We need to state that the African Orthodox leadership in Kenya had a very close connection with the general political movements in central, Western, and Nairobi provinces and especially with KAU, later to become the ruling party today, KANU. Together they also formed the inner core of African school administration cadre: Gathuna, Mzee Jomo Kenyatta -the future president of the republic, Fr. Elftherios Ndwaru were among the first teachers to resign their positions in the Government subsidized missionary school system. They opted for the now in high gear and gaining momentum, African ran school system. Also, Gathuna's personal relationship with the ruling party KANU and especially its president Mzee Jomo Kenyatta, the father of the Kenyan Nation which was on all counts very good, helped to bring the Orthodox Church on the forefront of both national and religious limelight.

The location of the Scottish Mission Head Offices in 1920's was in Kabete, on the outskirt of Nairobi City. It was here in Kabete Scottish mission center that the decree went out ordering both teachers and parents to sign a declaration against their culture, to reject the female circumcision. At that time the entire Orthodox leadership was actively involved in the creation and administration of the Kikuyu Karinga Education Schools Association against the wishes of both the government and the missionary bodies. Among all foreign missionary bodies there was a respected understanding that there would not be less than a four miles radius separating each mission center from the other in order to avoid competition and fighting among themselves. What is more, the Orthodox was located next door from the Scottish mission. While the Scottish mission was in Kabete, the Orthodox group pitched their grass-thatched tent in Waithaka less than three Kilometer radius from Kabete and about two kilometers from Thogoto

Kikuyu Mission Center. This shows you how the battle for and against African traditions and culture raged between the Orthodox leadership and all the missionary enterprise in Kenya combined. The Orthodox stood for the upholding of that which was purely African in culture and tradition, and did all it could to undermine the missionary effort in trying to eradicate that which was believed by missionaries to be primitive and heathen practices of the natives. This strong traditional support on the part of this infant Church would later on lead to a lot of problems ranging from polygamy to drunkenness. Today we are still in the process of trying to come to terms with it and our young priests take to drinking and quote the Greek Churches and America as examples of good churches with good smoking and drinking priests. But the European scenario is quite different from the protestant Puritanism that gave birth to African Christianity and therefore the Orthodox Church. This is an issue that I feel must be addressed as soon as possible or we will completely lose ground on what had already been gained in terms of moral uprightness and stability of the Orthodox Church in Kenya in particular.

It was not a surprise for the Orthodox leadership then, when in 1952 at the outbreak of full Mau Mau battle and the declaration of emergency by governor Evlyne Barings, the entire Orthodox leadership was arrested together with Mzee Kenyatta and other leading politicians and sent to prison, where they would remain incarcerated until 1961, when Kenya was granted internal government, self-rule. All Orthodox schools, churches and properties were confiscated by the government and given to the friendlier missionary enterprises such as the Roman Catholics, Anglicans, Scottish mission and others. But Waithaika would remain the Headquarters of the African Orthodox Church for years until late in the seventies when after the completion of construction of the buildings by the gift of President Makarios of Cyprus and President Kenyatta, they moved to the present location of Makarios III Seminary, which also serves as the headquarters of the Orthodox.

The formation of the Orthodox Church in Kenya was therefore an African intellectual initiative and story. This story was deeply rooted in the Kenyan political and religious problems: issues of education, land, African representation in legislative council, issues of economic plunder, bad working conditions, poor pay to the natives, issues of race relation, foreign religious influence, lack of African leadership in protestant churches, and the issue self-rule. These are the issues which gave birth to the Orthodox Church. When, why and how may not be very clear sometimes but the facts lead me to believe very strongly that there was no other stronger motive to the foundation of our Church than education, freedom, both religious and political, and self-govern-ance.

2.3. African Independent Church Movements Become Orthodox Under the Protection of the Patriarchate of Alexandria and Canonical Questions

The question often asked is how did the Patriarchate of Alexandria receive the Africans of East Africa, who were both schismatic and her-etics, into Orthodoxy?[142] To answer this canonical question, it is only proper that we consult the fathers of our Church and canons of their synodal decisions, decrees, and modern historians of canon law. There are many ancient canons of the Holy Orthodox Church, which specifically describe the manner in which heterodox should be re-ceived into the Orthodox Church. These Canons are here listed for our private edification:[143] Apostolic Canons 46, 47, & 50, 1st Ecumenical Synod - Canons 8 and 19, Second Ecumenical Synod - Canons 7, 6th Ecumenical Synod - 95, Carthage 66, and St. Basil - Canons 1, 4, and 47. It has been the practice of the Orthodox Church to recognize the or-ders of the Anglican Church by economy only in cases where the

---

[142]F.B. Welbourn, *East African Rebels*, p. 80.

[143] Agapios & Nicodemos (Eds.), *The Rudder (Pedalion) of the Metaphorical Ship of the Catholic and Apostolic Church of the Orthodox Christians*, Translation by D. Cummings, (Chicago: The Orthodox Christian Educational Society, 1957).

Anglican priest wishing to join the Orthodox Church renounces his faith and totally embraces the Orthodox Faith.[144] This does not mean recognition of communion with the Anglican Church. Canonically speaking, by exactness, the Orthodox cannot recognize as valid, any sacraments performed outside of the Church.[145] Even after acceptance, such Anglican orders would be considered invalid if such clergymen remained faithful to their former faith. The East African schematics completely denounced their Anglican faith when they joined the Orthodox Church. There are many questions and formulas put forth on how to receive heretics.[146] As for the details on these formulas, I leave aside but only to say, that the venerable Great St. Athanasios of Alexandria in his second letter to his beloved spiritual son Ruffinianus, states that any of the Arian heretics who had persecuted the Church, and even had made others to espouse the same but wished to return to the True Orthodox Faith, be received with a pardon if they repent.[147] I lift up only this notion because it expresses the idea of pastoral care or the spirit of the law. I believe that the Patriarchate of Alexandria exercised this spirit in accepting East African fathers into the Orthodox Faith and communion.

2.4. The Question of the treatment of Anglican Church, Orders and sacraments

The recognition of the African Orthodox Church by Alexandria in 1946 raises the same canonical issues relating to Anglican Orders and

---

[144] The Very Rev. Jeronimos Cotsonis. "The Validity Of The Anglican Orders According To Canon Law Of The Orthodox Church," *Greek Orthodox Theological Review*, 3 (1957) p. 182.

[145] Ibid. p. 185. See also Karmiris John. "Ways Of Accepting Non-Orthodox Christians Into The Orthodox Church" *Greek Orthodox Theological Review*, 1 (1954), 38-47.

[146] Ibid. pp. 187 - 196.

[147] Agapios & Nicodemos (Eds.) *The Rudder*, pp. 763-764. This Epistle was read twice during the first Act of the Seventh Ecumenical Synod. See notes on the interpretation of the Epistle p. 765.

Sacraments. In the periods following the end of First World War, the relations between the Ecumenical patriarchate, Greece and Alexandria with the England Anglican Protestantism were very cordial.[148] Since Patriarch Meletios had been an extraordinary hierarch in the three countries and his activities both good and bad, depending on which camp speaks of them, are very well documented. Patriarch Meletios had been a good friend of the Anglican Church at Canterbury. His opinions on this issue are expressed in the writings of Archimandrite Panteleimon Chrysochou, his chief Chancellor, when he was Archbishop of Athens, the Ecumenical Patriarch, and later as the Patriarch of Alexandria attests to this.[149] Meletios had misread an earlier decision of the Ecumenical Patriarchate of Constantinople regarding the recognition of Anglican orders and so he presumed that, holy services performed on members of our Church by Anglican priests had been proven valid.[150] When he learnt that African Orthodox were Anglican schismatics he quickly wrote Spartas telling him that re-union of the two churches was now very close. He advised Spartas to rejoin the Anglican Church in Uganda.[151] Meletios was then in discussions with Anglicans on reunion, which seemed to be very positive so that a possibility of reunion was envisioned. Did the Orthodox accept the validity and authority of Anglican sacraments and recognize it as a church in the same way as the Orthodox? According to the views of Patriarch Meletios and his position on this issue as expressed above, the answer is yes. This brings in the whole issues of relations between the Orthodox patriarchate of Alexandria and the whole Orthodox

---

[148] The Very Rev. Jeronimos Cotsonis. "The Validity Of The Anglican Orders According To Canon Law Of The Orthodox Church," *Greek Orthodox Theological Review* 3 (1957) p. 184.

[149] Ibid. p. 184.

[150] Ibid. p. 184.

[151] F.B. Welbourn, *East African Rebels*, P. 90.

understanding from ecumenical synodal point of view. Cotsonis has very eloquently treated this issue in his above quoted work. [152]

For the sake of the record it is my position that it would not change a thing for us in Kenya today, whether the patriarch of Alexandria accepted Africans canonically or uncanonically. What would have been important for the Patriarch ate of Alexandria would have been to exercise love and pastoral care to neophyte Africans. This gesture is the practice of the spirit of the law, also called *iokonomia,* and not the letter of the law. It is clear that Patriarch Christophorus, who had by 1946 succeeded Patriarch Meletios, applied *iokonomia* in his reception of the East African schismatics. This is not a deviation from the experience and practice of the Orthodox Church of the ancient fathers. In the Second Ecumenical Council held in Constantinople 381, we recall that only Gregory the Theologian and his small parish of St. Anastasia, was the canonical and only Orthodox bishop in the whole of the Patriarch ate of Constantinople. The rest were semi Arian-Macedonian heretics. However, for the sake of the unity of the church, this council unanimously decided to do something extraordinary, it received back all semi-Arian bishops in Constantinople into the true church fold without much requirement. The only requirement was a verbal profession of the true faith and chrismation.[153] By this generous act, unity was restored, and peace achieved in Constantinople. In the present case the Patriarchate of Alexandria acted within the limits of the spirit of the law.

2.5. The Constitution of the African Orthodox Church.

The canonical question that interest Africans is, was the constitution of the African Orthodox Church understood by Alexandria? Or did

---

152 The Very Rev. Jeronimos Cotsonis. "The Validity Of The Anglican Orders According To Canon Law Of The Orthodox Church," *Greek Orthodox Theological Review* 3 (1957) p. 182-196, 4 (1958), 44-65.

[153] Schaff Philip and Henry Wace, *Seven Ecumenical Councils,* (Grand Rapid Michigan: WM . B. Eerdmans Publishing Company, 1974, p.172.

the Patriarchate of Alexandria study it before or after it accepted Spartas and Gathuna within its fold? It seems that in the excitement of the moment both parties lacked interest of trying to study and understand each other's position as independent entities. Had the Patriarchate of Alexandria gleaned more at the African Orthodox constitution, which actually expressed the African thought and understanding of its partnership with Alexandria, a lot of misunderstandings and conflicts could have been averted. Africans believed, and that belief stuck, that they were an independent Church. Even after modifying his constitution in the process of being received by Alexandria, Fr. Spartas wrote:

> African Greek Orthodox Church shall be controlled by Africans, under the supervision and guidance of the holy Ghost through the spiritual, physical and fraternal help and protection of the holy see of Alexandria, Egypt. It shall be an absolutely independent Church in all her internal administration[154]

The Greek Orthodox Archdiocese of America states in its Charter Article one, preamble, that "it is a province within the territorial jurisdiction of the most Holy Apostolic and Ecumenical Patriarchal throne of Constantinople."[155] It makes its position within the Ecumenical Patriarchate very clear. Spartas believed himself to be the sole ruler of the African Orthodox Church governing with and help of the Holy Spirit. He saw Alexandria only as a good will supporter and fraternal protector. This is a major statement in terms of policy of governance and in terms of canonical understanding of what the Orthodox Church is all about. It is my conviction that African leaders never understood the ecclesiastical canonical meanings of the patriarchate of Alexandria being their direct administrator, on one hand and on the other, their own role in it. If they did understand their roles and their relationship with

---

[154]Ibid. p. 83 - Unpublished constitution of the AGOC, filed with the Government of Kenya in 1968.
[155] Charter Of The Greek Orthodox Archdiocese Of North And South America, TDS, (Brookline, Mass HCO Press, 1978), P. 1

Alexandria clearly, my intuition is that they ignored it or intentionally decided that the African cause in it was paramount to all other canonical requirements. Even though the African leaders, Spartas and Gathuna, were educated men of their times, they were not educated in theological matters and therefore did not understand their canonical obligations.

At that time of early 1920s the Anglican Church in England and the Orthodox in Alexandria had a dialogue going on, which was thought to be going to yield some good fruits soon in terms of possible union of the two churches. This made Alexandria to be both reluctant in accepting Africans under its wings, seeing they had broken from the Anglican Church and not being sure whether to let them in or not.[156] That is why from 1933 when Reuben Spartas made his application to Patriarch Meletios requesting to be received in the Orthodox fold, he would not be received until 1946. Meletios was cautious and conducted some secret check out inquiry about Spartas via the Anglican Church.[157] On learning that the group was Anglican schismatics, he advised them to rejoin the Anglican Church. It was tricky for all the parties involved, either way Africans were willing to entertain the idea of, not re-acceptance back into Anglicanism, but reunion with the Anglican as an Orthodox Church, not as a repentant prodigal son. This, the Anglican Church could not accept. It was only after Meletios had died that the new patriarch Christophoros, reopened with Situart, the new Anglican Archbishop of Uganda, question of founding a mission Church in Uganda.[158] Again the reasons that led Alexandria to finally accept African Anglican schematics to become canonical Orthodox was not canonically prudent or were not a spiritual desire to shepherd them, or reach out to black Africa. It was not even a mission strategy by Alexandria to expand its mission efforts in the southern frontiers

---

[156] The African Greek Orthodox Church, *The Orthodox Word*, July-August 1968, p.170.
[157] F.B. Welbourn. *East African Rebels*, p. 90.
[158] Ibid. p. 90.

to incorporate black Africans. But rather strangely enough, it was an effort by Alexandria to circumvent and out-maneuver the Roman Catholic efforts of missionary work by stopping the African schematics from joining the Roman Catholic Church. The Patriarch of Alexandria wrote to Archbishop Stuart with the primary intention of preventing the secession of the natives to the Roman Catholics.[159] Secondly the Anglican church had protested to Alexandria about the ongoing schism in their church, calling itself Orthodox and claiming to be affiliated to Alexandria. This did not argue well for the ongoing relationship between the Anglican in England and the Orthodox in Alexandria.

Independence within traditional canonical Orthodox Churches is understood to mean a local Church or provincial or patriarchal jurisdiction. Simply put, it is a church exercising freedom and powers, of governance of its local affairs within spheres of its canonical borders without outside interference, from neighboring or other canonical orthodox jurisdictions. Such a Church possesses powers to organize and administer it affairs: elect, ordain and consecrate its own bishops and Metropolitan or Patriarch. The Orthodox eparchy of East Africa is a subordinate Archdiocese and it is far from anything like even semi-autonomy in terms of its jurisdictional relation to the patriarch ate of Alexandria. But the problem of independence of this church stems from a perceived authority as opposed to actual authority. Why is this the case? Apart from occasional visitations by a metropolitan, the leaders of the Orthodox Churches in East Africa were in practice independent. They ran their own show with little or no supervision at all from Alexandria. Indeed, it was only in the late sixties with the arrival of Metropolitan Nicodemos in 1969, that we had a resident metropolitan in east Africa. Immediately after metropolitan Nicodemos was posted to Kenya as the presiding hierarch, we have the first signs of trouble shooting up with the disagreement between Bishop

---

[159] Ibid. p. 90.

George Gathuna of Kenya and the new Metropolitan over menial issues because there were no administrative rules and guidelines. The
Charter of the Greek Orthodox Church of America is clear; Articles: 1).
Preamble, 2). Purpose, 3). Jurisdiction, 4). Organization, 5). Administration etc.[160] African leaders, who since the foundation their
Church were unsupervised by any authority and were now bishops,
suddenly found themselves answerable to a metropolitan, who was
not familiar with African ways. Article VI of the Charter of GOCA
states the authority of the synod of Bishops and VII clearly states the
rights and responsibilities of the Archbishop, while Article VIII, the
rights and responsibilities of Bishops.[161] This is completely absent in
the Orthodox Archbishopric of Irinoupolis or that African Orthodox
Church.

It is my argument that protestant upbringing influenced African
leadership in drawing their constitution, and that the whole
protestant spirit, it seems to me, had confused their understanding of
Orthodox canon law and ecclesiastical terminology. We are reminded
of the limitation of their theological training that the African church
faced. So, if we keep this in mind, some of the mistakes and problems
that African Orthodox faced may be understandable. Now a quick
glance at the wording of Spartas constitution, which clearly shows that
he understood what he was doing in terms of protecting the African
interest of his organization, within the new reality of being under Alexandria, you will notice that the language used is a commonwealth
style of democratic due process. This is borrowed from his western European protestant church mentality. The Orthodox Church, on the
other hand, did not and does not exercise democratic due process but
rather applies theocracy or to be more precise in our modern day language and politics, a totalitarian means of governance, where those in
power assume a kind of and want to be presumed to possess

[160] Charter Of The Greek Orthodox Archdiocese Of North And South America, TDS, (Brookline, Mass HCO Press, 1978), P. 1-2
[161] Ibid. GOC Of America, P. 2-4.

infallibility in themselves. So, with the kind of mind set of the likes of Spartas, on the part of African leadership, and the grim reality that lay ahead of them in the Orthodox Church, problems were inevitable. Alexandria was on a head on collision course with African leaders from the start. I move that because there was less enthusiasm or desire on the part of Alexandria to educate and train Africans in: doctrines, traditions, general church management, and canons as a preparation in order to pave way for indigenous church and leadership, no substantial mission effort went directly into African religious training and leadership molding. On this education issue Welch is of the opinion that:

> If the Church is to stand on its own feet in the future without any official encouragement, and without so many helpers from overseas in the key positions, we have to ask three more penetrating questions about training Africans for church leadership up to this time. First, have Africans been trained only to keep the church "ticking over"? Or have they been trained to do the outreach work of the church, presenting the Gospel to the people who have not heard it before? Secondly, have African leaders really been trained to reach the educated classes of Africans? The educated classes are to be the rulers of self-governing countries of East Africa. It is necessary that there should an African ministry in the Church with sufficient educated members to be able to minister to this people spiritually...the fact has to be faced that at present there are not enough African clergy who are themselves members of the higher educated class... Thirdly have sufficient Africans been trained to do the organizational work of the Church – so that they can keep the accounts of the Church, plan the spending of its money and find ways of raising more money to carry out urgent work? Have they been trained and given sufficient experience to hold together the mixed and sophisticated, "politically-conscious," congregation of the Church in large towns? Are they able to plan with strategy the wisest use of existing clergy over the country? Are they able to plan to deal with emergency situations like rapid growth of towns, displacement of populations through change of system of

government, and the need for a ministry to the rapidly expanding numbers of secondary school pupils?"[162]

The reality in the Orthodox Church in Kenya is that we have not over the years, moved forward in the lines of thoughts here expressed by Welch. The result of this negligence on the part of administration has been a feeling by Africans of being neglected; discriminated upon and total disregard of African causes and presence in the Orthodox Church.

Secondly the constitutions of both Reuben Sparta's and Arthur Gathuna's movements were flawed, very shallow and inconclusive, and therefore did not for example define the term *"ekklesia"* as a church, and its administration properly. A quick example is the African Orthodox Church of Kenya; its Constitution does not have a bishop as its Church leader but has a group of priests as its leadership.[163] It makes no mention of a bishop except that other churches may send their bishops to help. Of course, Africans could have done that intentionally in order to protect themselves from an overbearing experience of missionaries that they already knew about, but this clearly shows the grave defects that existed in the unity of *"ekklesia"* from the beginning and were not corrected. Again, when you read Kenyan African Orthodox constitution it clearly shows a massive confusion of terminology and total misunderstanding of the Christian faith. For example, the second Article of the constitution of African Orthodox Church in Kenya states that *The Head of the Church is our Lord Jesus Christ as directed by the Holy Spirit who brought the faith to Kenya and govern the Church through the consistory with instruments from the Holy*

---

[162] Welch F. G. *Towards An African Church*, (Nairobi: Christian Council of Kenya, 1962) pp. 14-16.

[163] Article 2. B. - The Church in Kenya shall be head and managed by some Canonically Ordained priests (who must be all Kenyans) who shall be elected by properly convened general meeting of all the Orthodox parishes in Kenya.

Bible and the Holy Orthodox mysteries[164] The Constitution should have been the first thing that Alexandria should have sought to correct as they brought Africans into their fold. It is my position that this constitution and its right drawing and understanding, confusing as it is in Orthodox terms, remains a big obstacle to peace in Kenya today. We must move to bring all the parties involved at the table to discuss these issues.

2.6. Relations Between the New African Orthodox Communities in East Africa, and Alexandria.

Did Alexandria understand the reasons why Africans had broken with the Anglican Church and what was driving their new search for acceptance and union with Orthodox Alexandria? It is not clear to me that they did. My intention here is to try to highlight some specific problems that led to the departure of the Orthodox leaders namely: Spartas, Gathuna, Bassajakitalo, and Mulamula, from their former churches and the formation of the Orthodox Church. Our leaders need to know these factors in order to be ware so that we can prevent the same from happening to the Orthodox Church in Kenya. Africans broke away from Anglicans and other Protestants churches in protest against overbearing missionary influence, paternalism, subjugation, control and servitude.[165] They wanted more freedom of governing their own religious affairs, free from foreign influence. They also fought very hard for political freedom and still remain firm and truthful to the tenets of freedom struggle. As they joined the Orthodox Church, they hoped to enjoy all the principles they fought for, which were believed to be preached in the truth of Christ. They believed in the very principles of freedom of the oppressed that Christ and the early Apostles preached. Here in the Orthodox Church, they hoped to

---

[164] The African Orthodox Church of Kenya Constitution and Rules Amendments Article 2: The Head of the Church.
[165] Bruce Berman, *Control Crisis in Colonial Kenya*, (London: James Curry, 1990, pp. 128-129, p. 200.

meet Christ's preaching, teaching and charity in practice. Ogot stated that:

> "Anglican missionaries working in Kenya continued: during the inter-war periods, to subscribe nominally to a policy, which they knew could not be implemented without causing a serious political upheaval in the country. The white settlers were still clamoring for a Southern Rhodesia type of Constitution... some missionaries argued it was unnecessary to train African clergy... the missionary therefore continued to run the Church in their own way." [166]

Almost every year we have had problems with the ruling hierarchy ranging from revolts against bishops to push and chasing the Archbishop from Kenya. This is because the practice in the Orthodox Kenya needs to be injected with more charity. And so, after many years within the patriarch ate of Alexandria Africans seem to have failed to find, the love and preaching of Jesus Christ in practice or the idea of charity that was lacking in the Anglican Church that they fled from. If Alexandria would have understood these tenets and tried to deliver on them, then most if not all problems encountered thus far in the Orthodox Church in East Africa and in Kenya in particular, could have been avoided.

---

[166] B. A. Ogot, "The Church of Christ in Africa" *A Place To Feel At Home*, (Nairobi: Oxford Un. Press, 1966), p. 22.

> Chapter 3

3. AFRICAN ORTHODOX CHURCH GROWTH AND MISSION EFFORTS

3.1. Growth and Mission Efforts

THE AFRICAN ORTHODOX Movements in both Uganda and Kenya were founded as Independent Church Movements and would remain so until 1946, when they were officially received into the canonical Orthodox fold, under the wings of the Greek Orthodox Patriarchate of Alexandria.[167] At least in words and on papers it appeared so. I argued in this paper that the independence question was never understood clearly by both Alexandria and African leadership. That this issue was not explicated properly is evidenced in the trouble that led to both Bishops Spartas and Gathuna dying in disgrace, either in suspension, as was the case with Spartas or defrocked in the case of Bishop George Gathuna of Nitria. It is my position that their difference with Alexandria sprouted from the misunderstanding of independence factor. The difficult question for Alexandria to grasp was what that reception meant for Africans. Africans seem to have thought that they were received as a Church with some say or powers

---

[167] Norman A. Horner, "An East African Orthodox Church", *The Journal of Ecumenical Studies.* pp. 222-223.*?*

if not complete authority. Did the Africans know the extent of perimeters of their rule or the sphere of their authority as far as day-to-day governance of the Church in East Africa was concerned? It is doubtful that they understood their responsibility well because the Africans did not have any training in matters of canon law, theology, ecclesiastical order and the source of authority of the bishop. It is one thing to tell one that you must obey the Patriarch because he is our head of the Church. It is quite another thing to train someone in matters of canon law and equip him with the knowledge of right and wrong, the do's and don'ts and why. Being a traditional and canonical ancient Church under the direct authority of the patriarch and therefore cherishing the idea of order and obedience, Alexandria assumed on its part that the African leadership would understand and obey this order of things. What Alexandria failed to understand was that Africans were not used to that way of governance or did not know it indeed they did not want to know or care for it. The only instruction they received was how to officiate in divine mysteries, the liturgy, marriages and burials. They would operate in their own ways and styles befitting what they perceived to be right and honorable a thing to do. The idea of obedience to the patriarch ate in strict sense was lacking. There was no official means of direction and communication on regular basis with Alexandria. The means of transportation then was largely by steamship and took weeks and months even for mail to arrive. The appointment of a metropolitan to oversee East Africa was rather a symbolic gesture on the part of Alexandria.[168] It did not imply at first

---

[168] Norman A. Horner. An East African Orthodox Church. *The Journal of Ecumenical Studies.* pp. 224-225.

In 1958, East Africa formally became the Archdiocese of Irinoupolis in the Patriarch ate of Alexandria. It was assigned to the administration of Metropolitan Nicholas Varelopoulos, who continued to reside in Egypt but made periodic visits in East Africa to Ordain priests and attend to the other ecclesiastical duties.

real and actual administration, though Metropolitan Nicholas did visit East Africa. The new Metropolitan did not reside in East Africa. The liturgical and pastoral spiritual needs of the communities in East Africa continued to come from and be administered by both Spartas and Gathuna. In simple terms these two priests ran their own show undisturbed, until the late sixties and early seventies when things changed suddenly. The flock in East Africa knew these two and no one else. It will be understandable then, when problems set in. So that we can appreciate the fact that the communities in East Africa saw the suspension of these two and later the defrocking as outside interferences rather than church discipline meted on some culprit and renegade bishops.[169] Here we see lack of leadership direction, guidance and thus a faulty start for the Orthodox in East Africa.

3.2. The Success of African Leadership in Missionary

Once the Orthodox Church had come into existence our African leadership set to work in earnest. From about 1924 – 1946, the Orthodox Church grew in lips and bounds. The efforts of Reuben Sebanjja Spartas and Obadiah Bassajja Kitalo in Uganda and Arthur Gathuna in Nairobi and Matthew Mulamula in Western Kenya, among few others, saw the church grow steadily in numbers. One Article called it "perhaps the most remarkable Orthodox Mission of the 20th Century: a spontaneous working of the Holy Spirit that may... sweep the continent of Africa."[170]

These African leaders did not receive moral or personal financial help from any foreign missionary agency or traditional Orthodox Churches. But they struggled traveling many distances and covering

---

[169] B. A. Ogot, The Church of Christ in Africa, P. 65. The Anglican Church in Western Kenya experienced similar problems between African leadership and the mission office, which resulted in expulsions of leading members of the group from the Church and the formation of a new Church of Christ in Africa in 1957.

[170] The African Orthodox Church, *Orthodox Word*, July-August 1968. p. 163.

hundreds of miles to evangelize Africa. As we already mentioned they did not have much theological training but the little they knew they hurried forth to share it with their flocks. The spread of the Orthodox Church was steady and very successful in the early years. Their success was based on protestant mission modals that our elders had inherited from the Anglican and the Presbyterian Churches but tuned to the African needs and context that they knew well. They used the Orthodox freedom of the Gospel expression in local cultures and languages. In both Kenya and Uganda our leaders applied culture as their launching pad for Orthodox Faith. They raised similarities of Orthodox Church to African traditional practices and exalted those aspects, which appealed to African culture, social standing, age groups, traditional observance and purity of traditional leaders. They used the local dialects and local imagery and culture in their own limited way but were very effective in a way, in reaching the masses and appealed to them in worship, which was very similar to the African traditional worship. It involved traveling gathering communities and teaching them about the faith of Christ as espoused in the Orthodox Church. They contextualized the message of the Gospel to fit the African traditional cultural needs and context, because the Orthodox practice is similar in many ways to African traditional practice.[171] e.g. Baptism, is similar to the rite initiation or the rite of passage, priest performing liturgy is very similar to African ritual sacrifice and offerings, the priest standing before the Holy Altar is very similar to traditional African oracle priest standing before sanctuaries of gods and the aboard of the spirits. The sacrament of Penance is also very similar to the ritual of cleansing especially before going through the rite of circumcision, where initiates confess to the elders who have kept the purity of faith.[172] It was thus easy for our church fathers in Africa to draw comparisons, and examples from both, and argue that the Orthodox

---

[171] Mbiti John S, *African Religion and Philosophy*, pp. 58-73.
[172] Alyward W. F. Shorter, *African Culture & The Church*, pp. 122-128.

Church was the Church of our ancient African fathers, rooted in our African ritual and tradition.

Another element that contributed to the success of the Orthodox Church was its status as an instrument of a social cause and advocate for change. The Orthodox Church a rose as a social movement provoked by the rising hardships in both religious and political life in British colonial East Africa. Its pledges in its very early days were promises of change in governance of African affairs, to deliver freedom of religious observance, freedom from the missionary influence and interference in African matters, land problem, and even freedom of independence.[173] It thus saw itself as an instrument of hope in a very desperate situation where African life and meaning of human sanctity had severely been disrupted and undermined by the settler discriminative, racist politics and policies. There certainly existed a deep and unfulfilled spiritual, religious, gaps and political needs in the missionary enterprise. New African movements such as the Orthodox rose quickly and seemed posed to fill this vacuum. Anderson states that these new African movements represented another option, Christianity more in harmony with traditional ways and with African political demands.[174] We need to stress that Orthodoxy is still posed today as the hope of the African continent especially now that we are faced with myriads of calamities and ailments such AIDS, droughts and hunger that is now more than we have ever experienced before. More people are leaning back on religion and especially African religiosity and they are asking questions about God and faith. They want their "why this?" and "why us?" answered. I believe that given the Orthodox close proximity to African culture it could be the answer to many of Africa's social and spiritual questions. Africans are looking up to the Orthodox, the

---

[173] Walton R. Johnson, *Worship And Freedom*, (New York: African Publishing Company, 1977), p. 29. Like the AME Church of Zambia, Orthodox Church in Kenya related well with nationalistic feelings and supported the ideals of freedom fighters.

[174] William B. Anderson. *The Church in East Africa*, p. 122.

Church of the fathers, for answers. Can the Orthodox Church deliver on this? The Orthodox Church seemed then, to make good on its promises when it built schools and Churches and started to provide for other social amenities such agitation for clean drinking water, building of orphanages, sanitary hygiene and health clinics. By so doing it proved that it could give solutions to existing African social problems of education, societal concerns, and culture besides providing spiritual nourishment. It stood firm for African education, for both men and women. It emphasized the fundamental African practices such as female circumcision, polygamy, and traditional weddings.175 These practices had been painted by the missionary policies as heathen and unworthy of Christian observance. This bold stand on the part of the Orthodox Church found favor with the majority of Africans, who abandoned their missionary churches to join an apparently more tolerant and hospitable Orthodox Church.

I would like to underscore the fact that between 1935- 1972, which I consider to be the era of first ordinations, conversions and mass baptisms, were also years that saw our faithful experience peace, harmony, and growth in the Orthodox Church in East Africa. This growth and success took place at a time of and in the midst of sheer poverty and untold colonial and neocolonial hardships. It is essential to state that like many of the present African indigenous churches, which do not have any external support, the Orthodox Church was then self-supporting, self- sustaining, self-proper gating and self-governing.[176] People contributed money to build schools, churches, clinics and paid for their primary school teachers and priests wages, even if it meant that a priest received two dollars a month. The people paid for the two dollars and I think that it is important for us to remember and ask ourselves why that stewardship cannot be done today. The Orthodox Church both in Uganda and Kenya experienced tremendous

---

[175] The writer does not believe in or condone such practices.
[176] B. A. Ogot, The Church of Christ in Africa. pp. 64-65.

growth numerically and organically ecclesiastically, as a thriving lively faithful community because of its able African leadership. This success could not have occurred without a strong leadership and elaborate mission agenda and strategy in place. In his study of Pentecostal movements in Central America, Peterson attributes the success of Assemblies of God in Central America, led by the movement in El Salvador, to efforts of indigenous leadership.[177] He compares this movement with other Pentecostal movements that had the blessing of missionary presence and financial support and concludes that the indigenous led movements were more successful and more stable. He adds that these indigenous self-supporting, self-proper gating and self-governing Churches stood a better chance of holding its steady growth.[178] The African Orthodox Church in its early days begun like and about the same time with, and resembled pretty much, the Pentecostal Assemblies movements that Peterson studied in Central America.[179] Therefore, we in Kenya and those involved in mission might benefit from the findings of the above-mentioned study. Basing his standpoint on statistical data of several research organizations, Peterson states that *"Religiously inclined persons contextualized Pentecostalism, adapting features appropriate to their circumstances, to make their Churches not only the region's largest expression of Pentecostalism, but also one of its most important grass-root social movements."*[180]

The Patriarchate Alexandria, unlike the American missionaries in Central America, did not invest in the great potential of the indigenous leadership capability in Kenya in particular. The traditional protestant European and Roman Catholic missionary house in East Africa in the

---

[177] Douglas Peterson The Foundation of popular, national, Autonomous Pentecostal Churches in Central America. PNEUMA: The Journal of the Society for Pentecostal Studies, vol.1.1 Spring 1994, P.23-24

[178] Ibid. p. 23

[179] Norman A. Horner, "An East African Orthodox Church" *The Journal of Ecumenical Studies*, pp. 221-222.

[180] Douglas Peterson, P. 23

1920's had a lot of trouble that gave birth to the Orthodox Church, but even then, a keen gleaning into the mission policies of some of these churches indicate a slow but progressive Africanization effort on the part of the western missionary. The irony is that just when these protestant churches were posed to get their freedom, African leadership, and independence, the Orthodox Church voluntarily placed itself under European control.[181] The Roman Catholic Church had paved the way to modern time African leadership in East Africa, with the consecration of Joseph Kiwanuka first African Bishop of Masaka, Uganda in 1939. The Anglican in Kenya consecrated Festo Olang bishop in 1955, as Assistant Bishop of Mombassa. The protestant policy saw Africanization as an essential component of its leadership, at least as far as its missionary work and evangelism was concerned and it did make good on this.[182] Bishop Olang rose to become the first African Archbishop of the Anglicans in Kenya. Also, the Catholics were quick to realize the importance of indigenous African leadership in Kenya, and consecrated Maurice Otunga as Bishop in 1957.[183] Otunga would rise to become the first African Cardinal in Kenya and Archbishop of Kenya. Soon all the major protestant denominations followed suit but not the Orthodox Church.

In the Orthodox Church in Kenya the missionary has been successful in keeping Africans at bay from approaching the episcopate honor and has clung to the episcopate stuff and office. This is a problem and challenge for us in Africa in that the missionary has shortsighted vision for the future and he is there to stay. The Roman Catholic missionaries in East Africa made sure that "they trained an African priesthood to the level of the world, cosmic, priesthood. The result has been that the Catholic Church has produced highly skilled and

---

[181] D. E. Wentink, "The Orthodox Church in East Africa," The Ecumenical Review vol. 20 (1968), p. 32.
[182] William B. Anderson, The Church in East Africa 1840-1974, p. 143
[183] Ibid. p. 139

experienced African priests"[184] Our Orthodox mission on the other hand has been afraid if not apprehensive on the issue of African education.[185] The Orthodox Church in Kenya concentrates on training catechists and intellectually inferior priests unlike the competitive priesthood of the Roman Catholic Church. The mode of study applied in Orthodox Kenya is not an accidental one, but rather a calculated move to keep Africans at the bottom of the ranks of priesthood.[186] They can become priests to serve the tables, but not competitive enough to give their western counterparts a run for their money. The result of this systematic means of a well-known colonial divide and conquer policy, has led not only to the mistrust of the missionary enterprise in Kenya, but also to the disintegration of the Orthodox Church from within. The Orthodox Church in Kenya is not only divided but it is in the process of falling apart. It is very difficult I believe for anyone now to try to reconstruct our Church back to the past glories of what it was let's say 25 years ago. I submit that the Orthodox situation is now war-like and comparable to the British colonial Kenya situation in 1930-1960. Where settler and missionary community tried all the known tactics to hold Africans from having a share in the running of the nation and took away from Africans the best escarpment highlands of the rift valley and prime agricultural land for themselves.[187] This in effect was denying Africans their political rights, rights to land ownership, right to African culture, free worship, and rights to their very livelihood. In the Orthodox Church in Kenya today the missionary has taken everything into his hands and his hold on its leadership is firmly secured for him today and for his noble and spiritually elect generation

---

[184] Ibid. p. 142

[185] *The Church & Revolution in Rwanda*, (Nairobi: African Publishing Company, 1977), pp. 152-155.

[186] Our Orthodox Seminary was established way back in 1966 to train priests at the catechetical level. Almost four decades later the mode or method and scope has remained the same.

[187] F. B. Welbourn, *East African Rebel*, pp. 81-143.

of the future. Referring to that dark colonial period in Kenya of 1930's and 1960's Huxley and Margery write:

> All the lesson of the last few years seem to teach that a country is doomed unless it can achieve a certain degree of national unity, transcending barriers of religion, race or class. I can't imagine a harder task than this in Africa, and yet as I've already suggested, it has got to be faced. A measure of unity can only be achieved, I suppose, by a long, slow process of tightening the strands that pull communities together, and throwing, patiently and persistently, slender bridges over gulfs that divide- especially the gulf of race.[188]

Can we in the Orthodox Church in Kenya today achieve unity, free of racial discrimination and I mean also African against white? Though the above quoted words refer to the British colonial Kenya and, yet every beat of it expresses so eloquently the missionary verses African situation in the Orthodox Church in Kenya today. Can Africans be ready to forgive and set a new course of love, communion, and peace in Christ Jesus in Kenya? Let us pray that God will enable us all to come together in collegial unity.

As early as 1929 the Roman Catholic Church, through the Pope, had declared Africanization of its Archdiocese leadership in Africa as it goal.[189] This was so because during and after the First World War Rome was quick to read the signs of the times as to where forces of evangelism and colonial era were leaning and therefore calling Rome to act quickly in anticipation of the changes that were eminent. The Roman Catholic made it its policy to have equality in its priesthood. It declared from the beginning that *"there is one priesthood in the Church"*[190] and it made sure that this rule was implemented. There may have been many problems related to this and may be even today the Roman

---

[188] Elspeth Huxley & Margery Perham, *Race and Politics in Kenya*. First Published in London Mcmxliv, P. 168.

[189] William B. Anderson. The Church in East Africa 1840-1974, p. 139.

[190] Ibid. p. 142.

Catholic clergy faces some problems of race in its priesthood, but its leadership made it clear that all priests were equal. In the Anglican Church- C.M.S: "a policy had been formulated by Henry Venn, its Secretary from 1841 to 1872. This policy aimed at setting up as quickly as possible self-supporting, self-governing and self-propagating Churches overseas."[191] Why did Henry Venn come up with this daunting policy? Ogot writes that Venn and others like him realized that the church could never hope to make a permanent contribution in Africa and Asia unless it became an indigenous institution.[192] In western Kenya this task was left in the hands of two prominent people, Bishop Willies, later Bishop of Diocese of Uganda, and Archdeacon Owen to implement. The two prelates have left behind an inedible mark in the Diocese of Mombassa, in the Deanery of Western Kenya, later transferred to the diocese of Uganda. Ogot adds that *In East Africa it was only in Uganda that a serious attempt was made, under the dynamic and far-sighted leadership of Bishop Alfred Tucker, to implement Venn's Policy.*[193]

In the Orthodox Church, an African priest has remained inferior to the missionary clergy and indeed he is treated as inferior, though be he with equal rank with his mission counterpart. Andersen says that "The importance of Africanization cannot be underestimated. Independent churches sprung up in some cases because African Christians believed African leadership necessary for genuinely African Christianity"[194] How can this be? When missionaries have little or no interest in such ventures, to impound on this dilemma, the suspicious activities of some missionaries raise the issue of their agenda, and longevity of missionary posts, and missionaries in Africa. How long should a church remain a mission post, before it can become self-supporting, self-proper gating and self-governing?[195] It is said that experience is

---

[191] Roland Oliver and J. D. Fage, *The Missionary Factor in East Africa*, p. 220.

[192] B. A. Ogot, "Church of Christ In Africa," *A Place To Feel At Home*, p .21.

[193] Roland Oliver and J. D. Fage, *The Missionary Factor in East Africa*, pp. 219-22.

[194] Ibid. p. 145.

[195] A.D. Tom Tuma & Phares Mutibwa, *A Century of Christianity in Uganda*,

the best teacher, but even with experiences that abounds around us, which our Orthodox missionaries could learn from, no one seems too interested in such policies. There is a story told by William B. Anderson, that in those early Protestant missionary days:

> One missionary in western Kenya used to insist on being carried across all streams by his African servants. His African carrier got tired of providing the service. So in the middle of one river, the carrier arranged to slip and fall down, throwing the missionary into the stream... the missionary never asked to be carried again.[196]

Orthodox Christians have carried the missionary a cross many raging rivers. The above missionary story beautiful explains the African position in the Orthodox Church in Kenya if not Africa today. Writing about lack of canonical unity in Orthodox witness in Diaspora, John Meyendorff makes a very strong point on the issue of mission. He states: *"My contention - based, I believe, on unquestionable biblical evidence- is that as long as these communities understand themselves as diasporas, they will be unable to fulfill their mission as Churches."* [197] Orthodox mission church in Kenya today is repeating not only the mistake and confusion created in the Orthodox Diaspora of Western Europe, but also same mistakes of the history of Protestant denominations in East Africa from 1840 -1940's, when this problem of inability to learn from the past, and refusal to listen and hear Africans started to get out of control. The situation would grow worse until missionaries woke up to uncontrollable dilemma in the mid 1950's through 1960's. Anderson write that: by that time there were already a number of alternatives to this type of Christianity.[198] The Orthodox missionaries in Africa basically see the mission church as an extension of their own Church at home e.g.

1877-1977, (Kampala: n. p, 1978), 143-144, 152-154.
[196] Ibid. p. 118.
[197] John Meyendorff, *Catholicity and the Church*, (New York: SVS Press 1983), p. 107.
[198] William B. Anderson, *The Church in East Africa 1840-1974*, p. 118.

Cyprus in the case of Kenya for instance. Such a missionary effort is not, only, shortsighted, stagnant, and dry in terms provision of vibrancy of faith, but its faithful also become dependent and subordinate to the missionary and the Church of his motherland.[199] There is no chance of spiritual growth or numerical growth or structural growth, for in such situations missionaries, struggles to play survival tricks instead of evangelizing the populace with the true and viable Gospel of Christ.

African Orthodox Church leadership in Kenya in the late 1940's and 1950's formulated and applied hymns of praise to its war heroes in its evangelism efforts and emphasized freedom of culture in colonial Kenyan education to rally people to join them.[200] This created a real sense of community and of belonging in the African Karinga Orthodox Church. Peterson attributes the success of the Pentecostal Assemblies in Central America to its emphases on freedom of expression in worship and affirmation of the individual's worth within the community: provision of a versatile mechanism easily adapted to the variety of cultures, social classes and age groups.[201] In those early days of the Orthodox Church in East Africa, missionary efforts were implemented on the ground by African catechists, who were given short training at Namungona in Uganda and later at Waithaka in Kenya and sent out to preach the Gospel and to evangelize regions in East Africa. There was not one single missionary involved in the day-to-day running of

---

[199] Douglas Petersen. "The Formation of Popular, National, Autonomous Pentecostal Churches in Central America", *PNEUMA: The Journal of the Society for Pentecostal Studies*, vol.16, No.1, Spring (1994), P. 24.

[200] Gakaara Wanjau, *Agikuyu, Mau Mau Na Wiyathi*, p.53. The seditious songs 'muthirigu', praised African heroes and ridiculed European settlers, government officials and missionaries - an example of hymns and songs formulated to rally people to join the African cause and the Orthodox Church.

[201] Douglas Peterson. "The Formation of Popular, National, Autonomous Pentecostal Churches in Central America", *PNEUMA*: vol.16, No.1, spring (1994), p. 23.

the Orthodox Church in East Africa during that time, and yet the Church grew in leaps and bounds.

There were also settler community members of Greek descent visiting regions from Dar Es Salaam to Kampala and later became missionaries. Notable among this crop of missionaries was Nicodemos Sarikas, a farmer in the Moshi region.[202] He began work in Tanganyika about 1925, on arrival from South Africa, to minister to the Greek community in Arusha and some expatriates from Europe working in Tanganyika. He opened Churches in some bigger cities like Moshi and Dar es Salaam.[203] His legacy is today carried forth in the life of the International High School at Arusha, which is a Greek School founded by the efforts of his ministry there. He is also noted for giving instructions to the young Orthodox Church in Uganda at about 1932 when he advised Spartas to contact Alexandria and get the true Orthodox faith.[204] This was an on and off visitor encounter with indigenous Africa but that was it. Such ministries were largely not lasting efforts, Carl writes about the efforts of Sarikas:

> A Church easy to forget is the Orthodox Church. Its members were predominantly workers from Greece and other Eastern European Countries...even Africans joined...This input of indigenous Christians motivated a change of the name of the church to African Orthodox Church[205]

Looking back, I want to attribute that early growth of the Orthodox Church in East Africa to lack of missionary presence and involvement in the Orthodox Church life in East Africa. The coming of the Orthodox missionary saw the dawn of glorious helpful comforts but also brought

---

[202] *Orthodox Word*. The African Orthodox Church. July – August 1968. pp. 169-167.

[203] Carl-Erik Sahlberg, *From Krapf to Rugambwa*. Evangelical Publishing House, Nairobi,1986, p.140.

[204] D. E. Wentink, The Orthodox Church, The Ecumenical Review (1968), p.34

[205] Ibid. p.140.

with it evils of dependency, corruption and rivalry in the mission house.

Once the missionary came in, then wars of control and competition for missionary favors in forms of money, clothing and other fringe benefits stepped into the picture. The result of this seemingly healthy way of supporting Africans by provision of the much desired and needed social amenities was the dawning of accelerated immoral behaviors, greed, cheating, deceitfulness and corruption. The individual and collective efforts of our African people at work of mission and evangelism came to a standstill. All responsibilities and accountabilities fell and rested henceforth in the hands of the new and knowledgeable missionary. All the others had to seat back listen, watch, learn how things are done, and wait for the order from the mission office regarding all and everything.

During protestant missionary epoch in Kenya, Anderson writes that:

> Christianity's biggest failure was that it failed to meet the spiritual questions and needs Africans felt. It simply taught a new faith and worship, without dealing realistically with African religious experiences. Hymns were often pure translations from Europe and America.[206]

We are today experiencing many issues of and problems related to: lack of systematic education of our children and leaders, lack of social development initiatives, the uplifting of peoples social standards, divisions in leadership and lack of charity in Kenya, which calls for attention and solutions. The mission of the Church, John Meyendorff, again, tells us that it can - and should - always imply some accommodation and flexibility, as Paul made himself servant to all, that he might win the more (1 Cor. 9:19). The Church has always adopted their language and shaped her culture. Quite legitimately she becomes

---

[206] William B. Anderson, *The Church in East Africa 1840-1974*, p.118.

Serbia in Serbia, and Georgian in Georgia.[207]...and I add Kenyan in Kenya and Ugandan in Uganda. We need create to an atmosphere and room to enable us to accept that we need to re-examine our positions as a Church on issues such as the above and these here listed: Has the AGOC succeeded in developing a truly indigenous character?[208] Is there ground for hope for greater unity among presently fragmented Orthodox body groups in Kenya? Is our Orthodox Music satisfying our African needs or do we think it should be written in such a way that it would emphasize African lyrics, rhythms and melodies?[209] Have missionaries listened to our most pressing needs and problems? Do Kenyans in the Orthodox Church feel or experience fulfillment in it as a true faith of Christ? If your answer to any of the above questions is no, what should we do to correct this shortcoming? All of us that are involved in Kenyan Orthodoxy must come together to seek and find answers.

---

[207] John Meyendorff, *Catholicity and the Church*, SVS Press 1993, p. 108.
[208] An African Orthodox Church. Journal of Ecumenical Studies. pp. 223-233.
[209] A.D. Tom Tuma & Phares Mutibwa, *A Century of Christianity in Uganda*, 1877-19, p.145.

> Chapter 4

4. Challenges Facing the Orthodox Church in East Africa

4.1. The Birth of Archbishopric of Irinoupolis in 1967

WHAT WERE SOME of the challenges and problems that contributed to bad blood between Greek Orthodox missionaries and Africans, which would lead to the suspension and formal defrocking of Bishop Gathuna? His Grace Bishop George Arthur Gathuna wa Gatung'u was suspended in 1977 and defrocked in 1979 by the synod of Alexandria over issues of indiscipline. After his defrocking he severed his relationship with Alexandria in a letter he wrote to the Ecumenical Patriarch Demetris on 1st of March 1980, explaining why things had come to that painful epoch.[210] The situation grew worse, when there appeared two factions early on, one supporting Bishop Gathuna and the other Metropolitan Frumentios. There were many fights and a lot of blood was shade.[211] In this section we examine some aspects of what were the causes of the challenges and problems that have inflict a big rift in the Orthodox Church in East Africa over the immediate past two decades.

---

[210] His Grace Bishop Gathuna to His Holiness Ecumenical Patriarch Demetrios, 1st. March 1980.   DS

[211] Daily Nation –Kenya Newspaper No.6159, Monday, September 22, 1980, p.1.

It is my view that the birth of a company under the name of Archbish-opric of Irinoupolis[212] was the greatest canonical mistake ever made by Alexandria in the Orthodox Church in East Africa. This company was created in order to take care of Greek Diaspora in East Africa. The creation of the Archbishopric of Irinoupolis saw the genesis of divi-sions and splintered uncanonical ecclesiastical status of Orthodoxy in Kenya. While the East African canonical problems are different from the Diaspora of Western Europe and American canonical jurisdic-tional multiplicity, the reasons behind both of their formation are ethnicity, race, culture and discrimination. Since its inception this Archbishopric of Irinoupolis has continued to generate divisive poli-cies and is still today the cause and perpetrator of divisions in the African Orthodox Church in Kenya. One could argue that Alexandria in creating a company, desired to protect its Church assets in East Af-rica from greedy and vulture eyed enemies of the Church. That would be perfectly a right thing to do. That it is normal for a church to be in-corporated as a company. Well, could have held water and could have been true in Kenya, if the Patriarchate of Alexandria chose to incorpo-rate the existing African Greek Orthodox Church and kept its African leadership, since the title had been officially given to the newly created Archdiocese of East Africa by Patriarch Chritophoros in 1946. Has there been such an incident in the recent history of an Orthodox Church creating a new body within itself and changing its name and

---

[212] Archbishopric of Irinoupolis to Kenyan Government Company Act (cap. 486), Memorandum of Association, The Name of the Company (hereinafter called "the Archbishopric), DS, 29 January 1968.

All documents quoted in this section of the present work, referring to or hav-ing to do with Archbishopric of Irinoupolis Company, are numbered exhibits, officially certified documents of the Archbishopric of Irinoupolis, which were presented in the High Court of Kenya suit No. 3924 of 1987 in a case of Niphon Nicasious Kigundu Magu verses African Orthodox Church of Kenya. These copies were obtained at my request from the file archives of the High Court of Kenya by Father Paul Njoroge, the General Secretary of the Orthodox Church in Kenya and one of the listed plaintiffs in the case.

constitutional charter, which we can learn from? Yes indeed. The Greek Orthodox Church in America has had four different charters in her history, and the current one is now under review.[213] The first one was in: 1922, 1927, 1931, and 1977. But the Church of America came together in her struggles in difficult times trying to establish herself by forming new charters as needs arose in her history. It was not done by a few individuals operating outside, the scope of the official Church. Again, the comparison here is not a perfect match because in Kenya everything was changed, the including the name of the Church and the changes and the status thereafter, have never been reviewed by Alexandria again. As far as our Patriarchate is concerned, things are perfectly okay. There is a perfect statement of the Greek Orthodox Church in America, which relates to our situation in Kenya and, which justified the need for a Church to promulgate four different charters at different times to administer it. Dr. Lewis J. Patsavos writes that:

> Even though for a time adopting a monarchical administrative structure foreign to its essence. Nevertheless, true to Orthodox Canonical tradition of adaptability, the leadership of the Church recognized the need to return to its original synodal administrative structure. It recognized the fact that the reasons for which the previous structural change was initiated no longer justified its continued existence. It also recognized the truth that the Church as the Body (sic) of Christ can flourish only when all its members are allowed to exercise their various functions."[214]

Our Orthodox Church in Kenya is in dire urgent need of a new charter, which must adhere to canonical tenets and be true to our Orthodox traditions and, which will put an emphasis on reviewing of the past history of the current troublesome constitution and how to

---

[213] Lewis J. Patsavos, Edited by Miltiades B. Efthimiou and George A. Christopoulos, History of the Greek Orthodox Church in America, New (York: Greek Archdiocese, 198), p. 67.
[214] Ibid. p. 67.

correct it. The new one should endeavor to permanently entrench and incorporate in its; memorandum, and Articles of Association, the views and contributions of its African population. It is time for the Patriarchate of Alexandria to create room for our people to select a commission of inquiry to delve into the status of the current constitution, its problems, and anomalies with a view to overhaul it and come up with a new one acceptable to Africans. It is imperative for us to remember that all Christian churches in Kenya are charitable entities registered under the Societies Act as non-profit making organizations and not under Companies Act.[215] Our problems with the present constitution have immediately to do with the Directors of Archbishopric of Irinoupolis, who are all foreigners and residing outside of Kenya, except the Archbishop, and the painful question of only twenty Greek people registered officially under the Registrar general and accepted as the only members of Archbishopric of Irinoupolis. What is the Identity of all those hundreds of thousands of Africans calling themselves members of the Orthodox Archbishopric of Irinoupolis in Kenya?

All subscribers to the Archbishopric Company were not and are not today simple Orthodox Greeks but Greek directors of different companies. Again, the motives of the founders of Archbishopric of Irinoupolis were clearly spelt out, when later on in 1974, they decided yet again, to move to change the company from public to private.[216] The Archbishopric of Irinoupolis is now the official canonical Orthodox body in Kenya. This is not only strange and uncanonical but false and we must find a smooth way of getting rid of it and to correct the present a normally. Why is it that Alexandria has not been able to face this growing problem? Father Alexander Schmemann gives us the answer. He sates:

---

[215] See- The Company Act (cap. 486) license pursuant to section 21(1), TDS.
[216] Minutes of a meeting of the General Council of the Holy Archbishopric of Irinoupolis held at the offices of Messrs. Hamilton Harrison & Matthews, Nairobi on the 30th September1974, P. 1-2. DS

To be a canonical, one has to be under some patriarch, or, in general, under some established autocephalous church in the old world. Canonicity is thus reduced to subordination, which is declared to constitute the fundamental principle of church organization. Implied here is the idea that a high ecclesiastical power@ (Patriarch, Synod, etc.) is in itself and by itself the source of canonicity. But in the genuine Orthodox tradition the ecclesiastical power is itself under the canons and its decisions are valid and compulsory only inasmuch as they comply with the canons. In other terms it is not the decision of a Patriarch or his Synod that creates and guarantees "canonicity," but, on the contrary, it is the canonicity of the decision that gives it its true authority and power. Truth and not power is the criterion, and the canons, not different in this from the dogmas, express the truth of the Church.[217]

From the point of view of Africans, the title African Orthodox Church was not acceptable, and everything was done by Alexandria to remove this name from the picture because it is originally African. If you remove a canonically recognized Titles of a Church and replace it with something else, then in my view you have a sinister motive. It was known to Kenyans that the name identified the Orthodox Church in Kenya as African in essence and it stood for African efforts and ethos. The name Archbishopric on the other hand did not face any problems of recognition by the Patriarchate of Alexandria. Schmemann wrote that 'Everyone simply claims the fullness of canonicity for their own position and in the name of it, condemns and denounces as uncanonical the ecclesiastical status of others.'[218] One asks this simple question that if the Orthodox Church was already in existence in Kenya and dully registered under the societies Act as a none profit making Orthodox Christian Church organization under the name "African Greek Orthodox Church", why would Alexandria have considered to form

---

[217] Alexander Schmemann, "Problems of Orthodoxy in America", *SVSQ* 8 # 2 (1963), p. 69.
[218] Ibid. p. 67.

another organization to take over the running of the Orthodox Church in East Africa? Africans saw this move by Alexandria as a ploy to get rid of the African Orthodox Church and its leadership and in the process create a new church on racial lines. Was the Patriarchate of Alexandria's concern purely pastoral and a desire to see the spread of the truth of our Orthodox faith? Many think that it was an effort of security for settler community's interests, commercial enhancement and protection of their properties. Pulling all the pieces involved together one can be led, as Africans have, to a conclusion that Bishop Gathuna's suspension in 1977 and later defrocking in 1979, was a ploy orchestrated from Alexandria and that the divisions existing in the Orthodox Church in Kenya today were planned and deliberate. Whatever the answers are, the truth is that we are now a badly divided Orthodox community in Kenya, with three official groups all calling themselves *The Orthodox Church*. Referring to the divisions and multiplicity of canonical Orthodox Churches in America, Alexander Schmemann again states:

> To be sure there has always been divisions and conflicts among Christians. But for the first time in history division belongs to the very structure of the Church, for the first time canonicity seems strangely disconnected from its fundamental Content and purpose-to assure, express, defend and fulfill the Church as Divinely given unity... Truly we must wake up and be horrified by this situation. We must find in ourselves the courage to face it and to rethink it in light of genuine Orthodox doctrine and tradition, no matter what it will cost to our pretty human like and dislikes.[219]

I am strongly convinced that all our present problems in the church emanated and still emanate today from the creation of Archbishopric of Irinoupolis. The Africans verses Alexandria problems of the seventies were results of the growing suspicions emanating from the then growing mutual mistrust between the two parties initiated by

---

[219] Ibid. p. 68.

Archbishopric party. It is my argument that the introduction of this
company and its eventual taking over and holding of all churches,
properties and assets of the African Orthodox Church in Kenya, was
not only uncanonical and deserved canonical censor but was all illegal,
in very bad taste, and aggravated the already very tense situation in
relations between the patriarchate of Alexandria and Kenyans. In creating this company and purporting it to be *"the Orthodox Church,"*
Alexandria was not only failing to observe the ancient historical, canonical, and doctrinal tradition of the Orthodox church in mission,
but was also deceitful. This is the challenge that the Orthodox Church
in Kenya faces today, that of a policy of perpetual war of suspicion, rejection of African leadership in the church and a desire by Alexandria
not to listen to African grievances.

4.2. The Constitution of Archbishopric of Irinoupolis.

The Articles of association of Archbishopric of Irinoupolis Company clearly states that the number of its full membership shall not
exceed twenty people.[220] It further states that the choice of and inclu-
sion of additional new members shall be made by a decision of the
council members of the company and not through or by means of baptism. This clearly indicates that what we are dealing with here is not a
church but an exclusively executive member club of white settler community company directors of 1966. It is my proposal to Alexandria to
find a way to correct this problem in an amicable manner. Failure to
do so will continued exude strong waves of protests, which will continue to propel the Church away from peace and harmony in the
Orthodox Church in Kenya. It is my position that all the factors leading
to the foundation of this company and all the problems that came as a
result of its inception, were commercial in nature but affected and severely damaged the spiritual growth of the Orthodox Church in Kenya.
These problems took on, an identity of economic, racial, and political

---

[220] See Articles of association below.

overtone than religious or missionary endeavors because they are actually business cum political problems favoring one party against another. It is my contention that problems had been brewing since early 1966. The idea of a Greek Company was hatched by Greek businessmen in Nairobi in collaboration with Archimandrite Chrysostomos Papassarantopoulos, then the Vicar General, and acting with directions from and for the Patriarchate of Alexandria.[221] The result of this plot was the taking over, by Archbishopric Company, the affairs of the African Greek Orthodox Church, then ran by Africans, and replaced it completely with a new company. Why would the Patriarchate of Alexandria have undertaken to do this knowing that this was in canonical terms a very unsound and illegal a thing to do? I believe that the answer to this question lies in the political interest of the Diaspora and the business motive of the newly formed Archbishopric Company.[222] The political challenge for the Greek settler community in East Africa in the early nineteen sixties rested in the instability that western setters and business community faced within the newly independent African republics of Tanzania, Uganda and Kenya especially. These countries had gotten their independence in 1961, 1962, and 1963 respectively. After independence Tanzania quickly declared itself a socialist republic, in practice leaning towards communism of Russia, Cuba and China. In early sixties Tanzania embarked on the policy of Ujamaa or communes, where the state declared the nationalization, repossession of all privately-owned lands, businesses and assets. Policy of nationalization matured into real and imagined dangers, of victimization and brutal assault on individual and cooperates. This saw many foreigners lose property and ran for their lives. Kenya was

---

[221] He was a representative of the Patriarch- like the Roman Catholic Nuncio of the Pope. This took place despite the fact that; Patriarch Christophoros of Alexandria had in 1946, appointed Spartas the Vicar General in East Africa and Gathuna his assistant and vicar of the Orthodox Church in Kenya.

[222] Following is my reconstruction of the events leading to the foundation of Archbishopric of Irinoupolis.

feared to be heading towards a dictatorial regime. Many whites were gearing for the worse, but President Kenyatta saved the situation, when he quickly realized that he needed the white settler community, their expertise, industries and farm produce in order to keep the country on its economic footing. Between 1964 and 1965 Kenyatta did hold the famous Nakuru town hall meetings to reassure white settlers that all would be well, and that Kenya was going to remain a democracy. His appeal won the hearts of many white settlers, who decided to remain in Kenya and help Africans rebuild their nation. Uganda also was very unstable politically and the overthrow of the government of president Milton Obote in 1971 saw Idi Amin Dada declare nationalization of all farms and white owned companies, and asked foreigners to leave. This did not sit well with foreign landowners and big business companies in Kenya, among them Greek Orthodox who feared for a repeat a Uganda situation here. The majority of big farmland owner setters in Kenya and Tanzania were and still in Kenya today remains Greeks and Britons.

Since the Greek business community feared for what could befall them in such an event, they decided to protect themselves by registering their properties under a church body. This would have meant that they register their new company as none profit making Church organization, which would have made it impossible for them to do business under such a name according to the laws of Kenya.[223] In the Patriarchate of Alexandria's spirit of a policy of service for and protection of Greeks of Diaspora, Alexandria was quick to sense the danger a head, heard the plight of the Diaspora, and was willing to give a helping hand. A strategy was drummed up to have various Greek owned companies come together and register as one company under the Companies Act of the Kenyan Government but use a name similar to that of a church organization, which could pass undetected by Africans. This would allow them to carry out their business enterprises

---

[223] The companies Act (CAP. 486) License pursuant to section 21(1)

without much difficulty even in the event that these East African governments would try to nationalize whites owned industries and firms or companies. The church would not do this for nothing, it would be the trustee of these companies and have a say in the running of the company and a good percent of their income would go to its coffers. The Greek Archbishop would be the chairman of Archbishopric of Irinoupolis company and or the director. Later they settled on the church hierarchy being also the company secretary. This grand idea worked, and it has continued to work to the present day. Now let us examine some of the players and these challenges more critically.

It must have taken some time for the Greek community in Kenya to work out the models of operation for this organization before setting out to form an organization. This makes me put the dates of foundation between 1966 and 1967. The companies Act (CAP. 486) License pursuant to section 21(1) for the Company of Archbishopric of Irinoupolis was issues on 8/11/ 1967. It declares that:

> Whereas it has been proven to the satisfaction of the Attorney general of Kenya that: (1) The Holy Archbishopric of Irinoupolis hereinafter called "the company" which is an association about to be formed under the companies Act (cap. 486) as a public company with liability limited by guarantee and not having a share capital and for the purpose of promoting objects of the nature contemplated by section 21(1) of the said Act; (2) The memorandum of association of the company as approved by the Registrar of companies provided that its income and property whence over derived shall be applied solely towards the promotion of the said objects...Now therefore the Attorney General in pursuance of the powers vested in him by section 21 Act....hereby directs that the company be registered as a company with limited liability and with

the name The holy Archbishopric of Irinoupolis and without the word *"Limited"* being added to it.[224]

What were or are the objectives of Archbishoric of Irinoupolis? In part 3 of memorandum of association of the Archbishopric of Irinoupolis, it states that it is established:

(A) To carry on and promote in Kenya or elsewhere in East Africa: (1) the religious purposes of the Eastern or Greek Orthodox Church of Jesus Christ (hereinafter called "the Church"). Such work for the social and moral regeneration and improvement of persons who are destitute or needy as the Archbishop of Irinoupolis consecrated by the Greek Orthodox Patriarchate of Alexandria (here-in after called "the Archbishop") for the time being shall from time to time think fit and (3) such other charitable objects and purposes as may from time to time be determined or approved by the Archbishop for the time being.[225]

You notice that besides stating that it will carry out charitable work this major memorandum of the company does not say anything about mission and evangelism or of the spread of the Church of Christ or the Gospel of the good news. In other words, it technically avoids going into details that may unravel its actual objectives. But what is revealing is section (B) of the memorandum of association. It states:

In furtherance of the foregoing objects to do all or any of the following things: (1) To take over, hold and administer all property in

---

[224] Attorney General's office Nairobi to Archbishopric of Irinoupolis, The Companies Act (CAP. 486) License pursuant to section 21(1), DS, 8 November 1967.

[225] Memorandum of Association of Holy Archbishopric of Irinoupolis, Part 3, The objects for which the Archbishopric of Irinoupolis is established, section (A) (1 - 3), DS, 29 January 1968, p. 1.

Kenya real and personal, movable and immovable, which now belongs to or is held in trust for the Church."[226]

Now this is major because up until then, with the exception of St. Anargyros, which was built by Greek community of Nairobi and therefore was private and exclusively for whites then, all other Churches, church properties, and lands were donated, built or owned collectively by Africans. We keep in mind that the African Orthodox Church was a church which had been in place with a governing constitution since 1929. This memorandum clearly states that it shall take over, hold and administer all property of the Orthodox Church in Kenya. Section (B) (2) states that its object was:

> To acquire in any manner and hold for any estates or interest any property, real or personal, movable, or immovable, in Kenya or else where in East Africa and any rights or privileges in Kenya or else where in East Africa which the Archbishopric may think necessary or convenient for the promotion of its objects or any of them.[227]

Needless to say, the Archbishopric of Irinoupolis has acquired most if not all African owned Churches and properties including schools and Clinics and the rights of title deeds to the said properties. Money has been used to lure Africans to part with their title deeds. Now this is how it worked then and still it does today, in order for the Archdiocese to give aid to any community for any development, either to build a church or school or a clinic, it is a must for such a community to hand over to the Archbishopric of Irinoupolis the title deed of the land on which such a project is to be erected. Once the Archbishopric has received the titled deed, then they would proceed to give whatever money such a community needs for development. So, while the community rejoiced thinking that the good Archbishop had helped them erect a church or school, in actuality, the archbishop became the new

---

[226] Ibid. Part 3. Section (B). (1), p.1.
[227] Ibid. Part 3. Section (B). (2), p.2.

owner of that property and whatever building or structure standing on it. This is so by virtue of him or his company being in possession of the title deed to the said project or church. In other words, by accepting any help from abroad through the Archbishopric of Irinoupolis, Africans lose possession of what used to be their own. Can you believe this? This means that for generations to come Kenyan black Orthodox Church will remain slaves to Archbishopric company owners, who will continue to be actual owners of all the Churches in Kenya properties and assets there on. At first glance one sense no wrong doing but when you remember that no African, not even one, is a member of the company of Archbishopric of Irinoupolis, by its Articles of association, then you realize that in the event that this company winds up, as is stated in its Articles of association, that the Archbishop would sell or give everything to other charitable organizations, then we realize that Africans will be left empty handed by this treacherous design.[228]

What is more? The company directors swear that they will do anything:

> To maintain, turn to account, improve, exploit, sell, exchange, let, mortgage, dispose of or otherwise deal in any manner with all or any of the property or assets of the Archbishopric as may be thought expedient with a view to promotion of its objects or any of them.[229]

We have already said that the Archbishopric of Irinoupolis's purposes were and are today more of a trade and commercial oriented ventures than they are missionary endeavors. We are reminded that by design, Africans have no membership or positions in this Archbishopric Company and so they cannot have recourse to any forgone business or wrongdoing in business venture that it may be engaged in or undertakes. Here is what its memorandum of association says it will

---

[228] Ibid. Part 3. Section (B). (3), p.2-4.
[229] Ibid. Part 3. Section (B). (3), p.2.

do to further its objects: It will, *carry on any trade or business in the course of the actual carrying out of primary objects or purposes of the Archbishopric.*[230] In a nutshell, here revealed, are the primary goals or purposes of the Archbishopric of Irinoupolis company.

4.3. The Identity of Archbishopric of Irinoupolis

The companies Act (cap. 486) of the Republic of Kenya, memorandum and Articles of Association of the *Holy Archbishopric of Irinoupolis*, issued on February 7th 1968, is limited by guarantee and not having a share capital. It was and signed by Kaplan & Straton, Advocates, Nairobi, [231] January 1968. A Mr. Andrew Anthony Warwick, an advocate of the High Court, being engaged in the formation of Holy Archbishopric of Irinoupolis, made an application on behalf of Kaplan & Straton Advocates, Nairobia, to the Registrar of Companies, for a declaration of compliance with the requirements of the companies Act, for registration of a company, according to section 17(2), name of company being, Holy Archbishopric of Irinoupolis. This document is signed by, a commissioner of oaths on 29th January 1968.[232] The duplicate for file copy of Certificate of Incorporation No. 9 / 68 issued by the Registrar of Companies, states:

> I hereby Certify that Holy Archbishoric of Irinoupolis is this day incorporated under the companies Act (cap.486) and that the company is limited by Guarantee. Given under my hand at Nairobi this Seventh Day of February One Thousand Nine Hundred and

---

[230]Ibid. Part 3. Section (B). (4), p.2.

[231] The Companies Memorandum and Articles of Association of Holy Archbishopric of Irinoupolis, to the Companies Act (cap. 486) of the Republic of Kenya at Nairobi, DS, 7th.February 1968.

[232] Mr. Andrew In Anthony Warwick, For Archbishopric Company, to Registrar of Companies, DS, January 1968.

Sixty Eight. Certificate delivered to representative from Messrs. Kaplan and Straton. Date 20th February, 1968.[233]

Having dully been registered under the companies Act (cap.486), Notice of situation of the registered office or any change therein (section 108) for the name of company Holy Archbishopric of Irinoupolis was presented by Kaplan & Straton Advocates, Nairobi on February 7th 1968 to the Registrar of Companies: It reads:

> Holy Archbishopric of Irinoupolis hereby gives you notice, in accordance with section 108 of the companies Act, that the registered office of the company on the incorporation is situated at Valley Road Plot. No. L. R.. 1132/2, (P. O. Box 6119) Nairobi.

For the purpose of record the offices of the Church are today situation at Makarios Seminary but at the time of registration of this company it was at Waithaka, where the Seminary was located. The document is signed by Archimandrite Chrysostomos Papassarantopoulos, for Archbishopric of Irinoupolis, Secretary of the company and Vicar General. Date 24 January 1968.[234]

This signature of Archimandrite Chrysostomos Papassarantopoulos is very crucial and pivotal in assessing and understanding the Greek Orthodox Patriarchate of Alexandria's position on mission and church growth in Africa. In that it puts Alexandria squarely at the heart of the divisions that arose in the Orthodox Church in Kenya and points to it as the cause of problems that would later be generated from this company. History demands that Alexandria explain itself why it was so necessary for it as the Orthodox Church of Christ, to be involved in the formation of this infamous company. We are left wondering what

---

[233] O. J. Burns, Assistant Registrar of Companies, Certificate of Incorporation, to Archbishopric of Irinoupolis, DS, 20th February 1968.

[234] Archimandrite Chrysostomos Papassarantopoulos, to Registrar of Companies, DS, 24th. January 1968.

reasons could have steered Alexandria to get involved if it were not to undermine the African leadership.

4.4. Directors & Membership Of Archbishopric Irinoupolis Company

Who were the owners of the Archbishopric of Irinoupolis Company?

The signatories to the Memorandum of Association and Articles of Association of Archbishopric are the same people: bearing the names, postal addresses, and their occupations, and are the subscribers to Archbishopric Company. They are listed as the following:

1. Andreas John Stavropoulos, Director Magnum Estates (1964) Ltd. P. O. Box 9812-Nairobi,
2. Andre Aristidis Papadopoulos, Director Marwa Sisal Estate LTD, P. O. Box 6110-Nairobi,
3. Harris Lazarus Horn, Director Kenta Estates LTD., P. O. Box 7905-Nairobi,
4. Constantine Paraskevas Paraskevopoulos, Director Tassia Coffee Estate Limited, P. O. Box 9 Ruiru,
5. Phedon Eustace Meimaridis Director Meimaridis Limited, P. O. Box 5183- Nairobi,
6. Athanassios Anargyros Monnas, Director Monnas Investment Corporation, P. O. Box 5329- Nairobi, and
7. Rev. Chrysotomos Papassarantopoulos, Archimandrite, Holy Archbishopric of Irinoupolis, P. O. Box 6119- Nairobi.

This document is dully signed by the said subscribers and witnessed by Michael John Louros, Company Director Louros & co. Limited, P. O Box 3470- Nairobi.[235]

The issue of membership of Archbishopric of Irinoupolis is a thorny one. Article (3), Membership of Archbishopric, of Articles of association of Holy Archbishopric of Irinoupolis, states that:

---

[235] Directors and subscribers to Archbishopric, Articles of Association, DS, 29th. January1968, p.16.

The numbers of the Archbishopric is declared for the purpose of registration not to <u>exceed twenty</u> but the Council may from time to time register an increase of members.[236]

First let us try to understand that at the time of registration of this company, the Orthodox Church in East Africa was a living and vibrant entity, then at its highest peak of growth. Father Gathuna boasted of Kenyans joining his church in the thousands and predicted that it would become the national Church of Kenya. While Spartas also predicted that Orthodox Church would become the national church in Uganda. Of course, this was an exaggeration but even this explains his hope and optimism in the future of his Church. This shows us what the future projection for this Church in an African leaders' imagination was, and this is genuinely important for us who are interested in church growth, missionary historical trends, and projections. Articles (4) of association of Archbishopric of Irinoupolis even clarifies the issue of membership better when it states that "the members of Archbishopric shall consist of (A) the subscribers to the memorandum of Association, (B) the Archbishop or his Vicar General and (C) such other (if any) persons, being members of the Church as shall be admitted to membership by the Council."[237] What is important in this Article is the fact membership is limited only to those bracketed Greek officials of the company, which in effect says that admission shall not be by immersion into water three times, by a priest, in the name of the Father and of the Son and of the Holy Spirit. It shall not even be by the decision of the bishop who shall be the chairman to the company meetings, but by the decision of a council. Again, those who shall be admitted as members in the Company, shall themselves be at the time of admission members of the Church, implication here is by birth. So here we have a company within an already canonically established African Greek Orthodox Church and not wishing to operate within the

---

[236] Ibid. Article (3) p. 6
[237] Ibid. Article (4) p. 6.

parameters of this already established Orthodox Church but professing to take the Orthodox Church over, hold it, own it and do business with it in any way that the new company deemed fit. In canonical terms, I must say, even the most uneducated person would have known that this was not an Orthodox Church by doctrinal terminology and definition. But rather purely defined and bluntly put, it was, and it is a business company! The canonical error involved here is very grave. How to solve this problem is for me the greatest challenge facing the patriarch ate of Alexandria today. In this one problem lies a chance for peace and perpetual harmony and at the same time therein lies the grave reality of the possibility of demise of the Orthodox Church as a united entity in Kenya. It will take wise leadership and hard and unpopular decisions on the part of the Patriarchate of Alexandria and the ruling hierarchy to dissolve this company. This step, I believe, will be the hardest thing and toughest obstacle for Alexandria to overcome, and yet it could easily be the door to peace. I envision a breakthrough if the bitter pill is swallowed. A new name that could clearly annunciate our Orthodox Church faith would be something like *The Eastern Orthodox Church in Kenya"* or the *"African Orthodox Church"* or simply *"The Orthodox Church in Kenya: The Patriarchate of Alexandria"*; with no ethnic connotations enshrouding it.

4.5. The Growth of Archbishopric of Irinoupolis Company

The first Metropolitan to preside as the Director of Archbishopric of Irinoupolis was Metropolitan Nicodemos who arrived in Kenya in 1969. The articles of the company, given its character, hints at the possibility of there being no general meeting the following year, the year after incorporation into the companies Act. That would have been 1969, so the annual returns seem not to have been forwarded that year. So, the years 1969 through 1971 appear not to have had much going on officially in the company. This is hard to believe considering that the company had just got registered. We do not hear anything until the 17th of May 1972 when the Registrar General of the department of registry of companies, wrote to the Archbishopric of Irinoupolis drawing their attention to the fact that they had defaulted on forwarding their annual returns for the year 1970 & 1971 as was required by the Act. It further gave them a notice that if these returns were not furnished on or before June 1972, the registrar general would have no option but institute legal proceedings against the company without further notice of any kind.[238] What might have happened is that logistically it was impossible to run such a big a company from such wide margins of fragmentation and conflicts of interest in terms of differing businesses, parties and goals of the companies involved. So, it was expected that there would be some problems with management. Also, with the initial idea being that of camouflaging the real identities and business parameters of the companies involved, once the desired protection from the Church was achieved, the owners did not care much since they knew that they were covered. Attention could have been lost also from the point of view that many of the said members of the companies were planning to leave Kenya or were in process of resettlement. Even a further scenario could be that they expected the Patriarchate of Alexandria through its Vicar and Secretary to the company, to manage everything on their behalf but the church failed them. In any case the company had defaulted on its terms of incorporation in the companies Act and something had to be done.

The ruling hierarch was Archbishop Nicodemos who was then residing in Uganda. Now we remember that Spartas was supposed to be the general Vicar of the Orthodox Church in East Africa appointed officially in 1946 by Patriarch Christophoros of Alexandria. His home was in Uganda and technically therefore, the headquarters of the Orthodox Church in East Africa was situated in Kampala, Uganda. Anyway, while Nicodemos was in Kampala, and had just returned from Greece, he received news from Kenya, in which he already knew, that their

---

[238] Registrar General of the Department of Registry of Companies, to Archbishopric of Irinoupolis, TDS, 17th May 1972.

.

company had defaulted on filing its returns and that the Kenyan government was about to take them to court. Nicodemos hurriedly wrote to the department of the registrar general registry of companies on 3rd July 1972. Here I quote:

> "I have just returned to East Africa and I was handed your letter Ref.9/68 of the 13th ultimo sent to my Nairobi office. I have much pleasure in returning the forms for 1970 and 1971 signed by myself being the Director and Secretary of the Holy Archbishopric of Irinoupolis. Please acknowledge receipt of this letter to Box No. 747, Kampala. Yours prayerfully, Signed Archbishop Nicodemos".[239]

With this official letter of his Eminence Archbishop Nicodemos, dully signed and with official letter head of the Archbishopric of Irinoupolis and stamped with the official Kenyan government stamp of the registrar general of the registry of companies Act, we have our Archbishop committing himself as the Director and Secretary of Holy Archbishopric and Irinoupolis Company. First it is difficulty to grasp how it was possible that the Director and Chairman of a company was also its secretary. Already we can sense that this company was doing business in a weird way if not in a very questionable manner. But let us give it benefit of the doubt. The said return forms by Archbishop Nichodemos were not accepted as satisfactory filing returns by the registrar general of registry of companies. Instead they were sent back to the Archbishop by the registrar of companies with father threatening of prosecution. The letter from the Assistant Registrar of Companies to one of his assistants, a Mr. Kithyomi, states:

> You will notice from the file that the company has re-submitted to me the 1970-9172 annual returns, which I rejected vide my letter of 2ndOctober, 1973. The company has also failed to furnish the

---

[239] Eminence Archbishop Nicodemos, for Archbishopric, to the Registrar General Registry of Companies Nairobi, TDS, 3rd July 1972.

requirements of section 128(1) of cap. 486, could you please return the attached form 202 for the 1973 and threaten with prosecution.[240]

Meanwhile between 1973 and 1974 Archbishop Nicodemos was suddenly removed and by mid-1974 Archbishop Froumentios Nassios was the new Archbishop of Archbishopric of Irinoupolis. A meeting of the members of the Holy Archbishopric of Irinoupolis was held in Nairobi, with Archbishop Frumentios as chairman, on the 30th September 1974 at 10.00 a.m. Those present according to the minutes of the meeting of the general council of Archbishopric of Irinoupoli were, as full members: Archbishop Froumentios Nassios, H. Horn, A.A Papadopoulos, P. E. Meimaridis. Also in attendance were: A. D. Zagoritis, E. D. Zagoritis, A. M. Orphanos, Rev. Gabriel Nicolaidis, and S. A. Eastwood (for Hamilton Harrison & Matthews, advocates of the company).[241] A few things came up in this meeting. It seems that what went into the minutes was the official line of what took place but not everything that was discussed. To begin with the minutes do not give details but only that 1). Mr. Eastwood advised the council that by their constitution, the membership of the Archbishopric may not exceed 20 and that the members were registered as being a) The subscribers to the memorandum of association, b) The Archbishop or his Vicar General, c) Such other persons as shall be admitted to membership by the council. According to Our Orthodox teaching the only known means of admission into the *"Ekklesia"*, and by which one:

Becomes a permanent and legitimate member while at the same time acquiring the identity of a Christian is by baptism (John. 3:5)

---

[240] Assistant Registrar of Companies, to Mr. Kithyomi, TDS, 5th July 1974.

[241] Minutes of the General Council of the Holy Archbishopric of Irinoupolis, held at the offices of Messrs. Hamilton Harrison & Matthews Nairobi, TDS, 30th September1974, pp.1-2.

Elekiah Andago Kihali

-Except a man be born of the water and of the Spirit, he cannot enter the Kingdom of God[242] (see also Matthew 28:18-20).

The company advocate reminded the council that of the subscribers to the memorandum of Association, only Messrs. H. Horn, A. A. Papadoupolos and Meimaridis were still resident in Kenya. The other members having left the country, as I mentioned earlier that they were in process of resettling. The advocate of the company also reminded them that by their constitution their membership could not exceed twenty persons. We also note that when alerted that some members of this company had left the country, the council immediately voted to replace them with new members. In canonical definition of the Orthodox Church-Ekklesia is said to be:

> The divine organization founded by our Lord Jesus Christ for the salvation and sanctification of the faithful and guided by the Holy Spirit in order to achieve this end. It is composed of all who correctly believe in Christ as God and Savior of the world and united organically by the same Orthodox faith and the same sacraments into one "body" with the Lord as the "Head." [243]

Our membership in the Orthodox Church is permanent only in case where one falls to apostasy, may he be removed from membership and for those who die while in good standing they remain even in death, as triumphant members. Even in case of apostasy only a canonically constituted synod may declare such one no longer Orthodox. I bring up the definition of the canonical understanding of our membership in the Church to pose a statement that, what we have in this company does not resemble a church at all and that the fact the world is convinced that Archbishopric of Irinoupolis is a church, is itself confusing and a continuation of a long list of uncanonical adventures. The

---

[242] Professor Lewis J. Patsavos, Manual for the course in Orthodox Canon Law, Brookline Massachusetts, 1975. p. 50.
[243] Ibid. 1975.

truth should be told that while we carry on some good and acceptable charitable efforts in Kenya as an Orthodox Church, in fact we are by constitution a company.

In this same meeting of September 30th 1974, 2) it was resolved that the under-mentioned persons be admitted to the membership of the company, namely: a) Andrew Dimitri Zagoritis, b) Elie Dimitri Zagoritis, and c) Alexandros Mina Orphanos. 3) Mr. Eastwood advised the council that by its constitution it required no less than 5 councilors and no more than eight. 4) It was resolved that Messrs. A. D. Zagoritis, E. D. Zagoritis and A. M. Orphanos be appointed councilors forthwith. 5) Mr. Eastwood advised the council that the Rev. Chrysostomos Papassarantopoulos had died. 6) It was immediately resolved that Father Gabriel be appointed the Secretary of the company. 7) Alerting the meeting that proceedings were currently being brought against the company by the government of Kenya for failing to file its returns,

Mr. Eastwood also advised Archbishopric that, in order to avoid the filing of balance sheet in the future, the company should be converted to a private company and the council could see no reason why this should not be done.[244]

This being the case, the resolution was passed. It was resolved therefore, that Father Gabriel should call an extraordinary meeting of the company and should send out notices forth with.[245] That extraordinary meeting of the members of the Holy Archbishopric of Irinoupolis was held, again at the offices of the Messrs. Hamilton Harries & Matthews, Esso House, Mama Ngina Street, Nairobi on the 16th October 1974. The director of the general council, of the company, had called this meeting as an extraordinary General meeting. It convened

---

[244]Minutes of the General Council of the Holy Archbishopric of Irinoupolis, held at the offices of Messrs. Hamilton Harrison & Matthews Nairobi, TDS, 30th September1974, pp.1-2.
[245] Extraordinary meeting of the Holy Archbishopric of Irinoupolis Nairobi, TDS, 16th October 1974

in order to convert the Archbishopric from a public to a private company. This followed the advice by the company advocate in the previous meeting that they should convert Archbishopric to a private company in order to avoid filing the balance sheet. In this meeting the minutes item number 4 states that "it was resolved that, as all members of the company being present, that the annual General meeting of the company for 1974 take place immediately"[246] It is important I think to state that all the members of the company were present. This being a very crucial meeting in, which two important decisions were made, first it was decided to call a general meeting within the extraordinary meeting, which was in process, in order to discuss the conversion of Archbishopric from a public to private company. This motion was passed unanimously. Originally the meeting was called extraordinary and all members being present they decided to end the first one and embark on a general meeting for 1974, which finally decided to convert Archbishopric into a private company. This was a milestone in the short history of this organization and one, which proves my argument that this company was not and is not a church but a powerful business enterprise. The full list of the members is given in the annual return of the company on 30th October 1974. They are: Archbishop Frumentios Nassios, Andreas Aristidis, H. Horn, A. A. Papadopoulos, Harris Lazarus, Phedon Eustace, Meimaridis, Andrew Dimitri Zagoritis, Elie Dimitir Zagoritis, and Alexandros Mina Orphanos. And the company Secretary is listed as Rev. Gabriel Dimitiri Nicolaidis. The nationality of all the members is listed in the returns as Greek. While the Orthodox Archbishop of East Africa or should I say the Archbishopric of Irinoupolis – Archbishop Frumentios – put the total number of his Church members to be as the above-named numbering ten (10) people, black African Orthodox Christians were in the hundreds of thousands in 1974. By this time in 1974 Bishop Gathuna

---

[246] General meeting of the Holy Archbishopric of Irinoupolis Nairobi held immediately following the extraordinary one, TDS, 16th October 1974.

had put the number of African Orthodox Christians to be over (4) four million people. Though this was a huge exaggeration in the game of numbers for political purposes and gains, even this, Gathuna's ploy, was more credible, than the game of exclusionists.[247] When Archbishop Makarios III of Cyprus visited Kenya in 1971, he baptized more than five thousand people in one month alone. How could we then be diminished to ten people in a matter of a few months?

Secondly, we look at the reasons why the Archbishopric Irinoupolis, a public company, was converted into a private company. The registrar general had rejected the make-believe filing done by efforts of Archbishop Nicodemos, and later that of Archbishop Frumentios Nassios. A letter from the Registrar general's office in 1974 reads:

Holy Archbishopric of Irinoupolis, I return herewith the 1974 annual return for the above-named Company. The annual returns of the above company for the years 1970, 1971, and 1973 have not been resubmitted to me for filing. The first three annual returns were returned to the company vide my letter dated 2nd of October 1973, and the 1973 annual return, was returned to the company vide my letter dated 9th July, 1974. The relevant balance sheet should be furnished along with the annual return as required by section 128(1) of the company Act[248]

It was inevitable to convert the company into a private one in order to avoid the eventuality of its members ending up in jail. A case had been filed against Holy Archbishopric of Irinoupolis and its directors by the state in the Resident Magistrates Court in Nairobi, for failing to deliver an annual return to the Registrar of companies contrary to section 127(1) of companies Act, and punishable under the section 395 of the said Act.[249] It was obvious by then that the company was in a mess

---

[247] Who is who in Kenya, 1977.

[248] Assistant Registrar of Companies, to M/S. Hamilton Harrison & Matthews Advocates, copied to the Directors of Holy Archbishopric of Irinoupolis, Nairobi, TDS, 15th November1974.

[249] The state verse Archbishopric of Irinoupolis, The Resident Magistrates Court Nairobi Criminal Case No. 320, TDS, 30thJuly 1974.

and that the directors were having difficulty in filing its returns. These difficulties could have arisen from the fact that many of the first lot of members or subscribers or directors, (all these titles mean the same thing) had already left the country. And so, the company was struggling to regroup and get business running again. But even more important is the reason that we might not be thinking about, that the company was deliberately trying to avoid submitting its returns to the state in order to swindle the government off a lot of revenues. This is the most likely scenario because we have already stated that the company advocate Mr. Eastwood had in the meeting of the general council of Holy Archbishopric held on 30th of September 1974, advised the council that "in order to avoid the filing of balance sheet, the company should be converted to a private company and that the council could see no reason why this should not be done." This was done immediately with our own Archbishop Frumentios Nassios presiding over the general council. Nothing could have stopped this company from defrauding the state off millions of shillings. Indeed, the reason for converting the company to private is clearly to avoid paying tax revenue to the state. Again, we see that it was a difficult situation for the young company, where some members wanted out and were leaving for their motherland. This was an incentive good enough to make one not to file returns since they were leaving anyway. The government of Kenya at first refused to covert the existing Archbishopric Company into a private one.

The Deputy Registrar General of the registry of companies was even startled and confused on how and why the Archbishopric of Irinoupolis was moving to and or could move to convert itself into a private company seeing that it was a public company with a limited guarantee. On 7th July 1974, he wrote to the registry of companies through C.R. O (Mr. Sameja) expressing his doubts and cautioning them that the performance of Archbishopric company in the past had been dismal and wanting. His letter reads:

I have given some consideration to this matter and fail to understand how the above public company can be converted to private company without it first altering its articles of association. Perhaps you will also consider whether a company limited by guarantee and having no share capital can be a private company. I note that the past performance of this company has been unsatisfactory. The company has defaulted in submitting the annual Returns, balance sheet, etc. It is not practice of the Attorney General to grant license under section 21 to private company and we may have to recommend to the attorney general to revoke the license issued to this company. Would you kindly bring the above to the notice of the company and let us see what its reaction is going to be[250]

By 1975 no satisfactory returns of the Archbishopric Company had been filed with the registrar of companies since 1969. A letter written by assistant registrar of companies to the Archbishopric of Irinoupolis through their advocate Hamilton Harrison & Matthews reads:

I return herewith the 1969- 1974 annual returns together with the balance sheets relating to the above company. 1) The alterations relating to the years of the returns should be signed for. 2) The particulars of the persons who were directors as at the date of each annual return should be furnished. If any changes have occurred, the appropriate notifications thereof should be filed with me. Pursuant to section 201 of the companies Act. 3) The balance sheet should be certified true copy in pursuance of section 128(1).[251]

But in kind of a twist of events, the registrar of companies in a change of heart of sorts, wrote on 2nd April 1975 to Harrison & Matthews advocates for Archbishopric of Irinoupolis notifying them that *'I have to advise that the above named company has been converted from*

---

[250] The Deputy Registrar General of the registry of Companies, to C. R. O. (Mr. Sameja), TDS, 7th November1974.
[251] Assistant Registrar of Companies, file Ref: C.13294, to Hamilton Harrison & Matthews Advocate, for Archbishopric of Irinoupolis, TDS, on 15th March 1975.

113

public to private company. Its new registration number is C.13294."[252] From 1975-9180 the events that followed were horrendous war time like events, which need more study and synthesis before they can be documented. This will have to wait for documentation in the future.

Meanwhile problems had been developing between Bishop George Gathuna of Nitria and his deputies. This difference was fueled by forces favorable to Archbishop Frumentios, and by the ongoing development of the construction of the Seminary of Makarios III at Rirruta, which involved a lot money changing hands between parties allied to the major players in Kenya namely: Bishop Gathuna and the General Secretary of the Church then, Father Eleftherios M. Ndwaru and Archbishop Nicodemos and later Archbishop Frumentios. There was intense lobbying by different parties allied to these groups, for a share in the financial gains and benefits: working force, employment of new workers at the about to be completed seminary then, and eventual control of it. The details about these skirmishes are scanty but it is evident that in 1972, Bishop George Gathuna had a sharp difference of opinion in matters of practice and application in mission with Archbishop Nicodemos. Again, Arthur Gathuna had recently been made Auxiliary Bishop George of Nitria, and Africans saw him as their legitimate leader and wondered why he should bend so low in taking orders from the much younger Archbishop Nicodemos and later Archbishop Frumentios. The existing differences saw Nicodemos depart unceremoniously from Kenya in 1973. When Archbishop Frumentios arrived to take over from Nicodemos, he arrived with impunity and fixed opinion over how things were going to be ran. His relationship with Bishop George Gathuna never took off the ground and there was bad blood between them. The fact that, by now, Africans new that the money coming from abroad to build the seminary and help their Church was not going into the African Orthodox Church coffers or

---

[252] Assistant Registrar of Companies, Ref: C.13294, to Hamilton Harrison & Matthews Advocate, for the Company of Archbishopric of Irinoupolis, TDS, 4th February 1975.

account, but into the Archbishopric of Irinoupolis account, made matters worse. Gathuna was quietly pushed aside from the running of the affairs of the Church and instead Frumentios and the council of Archbishopric danced to their own tune oblivious of the feeling of the masses. Temperature between the two factions of Gathuna on one side and that of the Secretary General Father Elftherios Ndwaru and the Archbishop on the other side was rising and this gaining of momentum precipitated into an open conflict. Gathuna had early in 1974 decided to have a number of women dig the land at the newly finished seminary and plant some vegetables for the Church. The number of women employed to do this work was big and from Gathuna's own back yard in Waithaka. Technically this was a power game in the struggle for control of the Archdiocese or should I say for Bishop George Gathuna it must have been an effort to reclaim his lost glory in leadership. Word reached Archbishop Frumentios that Gathuna had put his people on the Seminary ground and that he was literally now calling shots there. The Archbishop was very upset over this issue and a big quarrel erupted between bishop Gathuna and Metropolitan Frumentios over this workers and labor issue. We recall Gathuna was a powerful public figure, one of the most senior Councilors of Nairobi City Council and an acquaintance of President Kenyatta. He used his influence to undermine the authority of Archbishop Frumentios and to crack down on his opponents. But the greatest mistake that Bishop Gathuna did in the process was to refuse the opening of Makarios Seminary. Once his people were kicked out of the seminary work force, and opposition was mounting against him, Bishop George Gathuna completely refused to allow Archbishop Frumentios to open the now completed beautiful Seminary built by the support and funding of President and Archbishop Makarios of Cyprus. Many priests were very upset with Bishop George over this, for taking this stand in his struggle against Archbishop Frumentios. In the mix up that followed this quarrel, Bishop George Gathuna Wa Gattungu of Nitria started to ordain some clergy without the permission of the Archbishop. This was

Gathuna's undoing, by this act he drew the anger of Alexandria which was already tired with him. Kenyan priests were also divided over this issue. Almost half of the priests were opposed to this idea not because it went against the authority of the archbishop but because he was ordaining people who had not gone through the seminary. Waithaka Seminary had been established since 1966 and it was the tradition of the Church now to have all those to be ordained priests pass through seminary training at Waithaka. Gathuna overlooked this seminary factor and went ahead to ordain some handpicked villagers without the blessings of the Archbishop or that of the majority of our priests. But his inner core of elders council or advisers seeing the present struggle between Gathuna and Archbishop Frumentios as the struggle for African leadership's survival, urged Bishop Gathuna to go forth in his present endeavors of ordination of the much-needed clergy. By this act war had started. What followed was a chain of events, which are beside the scope of this paper in terms of space, research and so will be treated within a later work. But these events culminated into Gathuna being suspended in 1977 and eventually defrocked in 1979 by the Synod of Alexandria.

4.6. A New Dawn In Orthodox East Africa

The next era of Archbishopric of Irinoupolis was the era Professor Acting Archbishop Anastasios Yannulatos. This was a time of peace and attainment to some level of unity and harmony in the Orthodox Church in East Africa, to a level that brought back respect and spiritual growth to the Orthodox community in East Africa.[253]

When Anastasios arrived in Kenya in1981 the problems of Archbishopric of Irinoupolis had grown to chaotic situation. The orderly rule of law and administration of the Church was in total jeopardy. The problems of Archbishopric were not about to end but were about to escalate

---

[253] Archbishop Anastasios was acting Archbishop of East Africa from 1981-1991.

with a new steam steered by a desire for control and greed during the time of vacuum created by the departure of Bishop Gathuna who had recently been defrocked and the demise of Archbishop Frumentios who had recently died mysteriously. Needless to say, the work of Acting Archbishop Anastasios was cut out for him. The task ahead of him was simply a daunting one. But he quickly got to work forging new friendships among the African clergy. He extended an olive branch to opposition group and even reached out as much as he could to Bishop Gathuna and African Orthodox Church officials. This was an effort to bring peace to the now fragmented African Greek Orthodox Church, now official known as Archbishopric and its bitterly divided factions. One faction led by able and defiant Bishop Gathuna, in exile of sorts, and the other was led by a very determined General Secretary of the official organ of Archbishopric, Father Elftherios M. Ndwaru and now allied to Archbishop Anastasios. As much as Archbishop Anastasios would try, it was a no-win situation for him in Kenya. There were too many insurmountable obstacles strewn along his difficulty path. First let us just ran thorough some of the most prominent once that I knew about and then we will try to sort out through the ruble and see if we can make out anything or come out with some reasons and suggest some solutions.

Problem number one was that the newly posted Acting Archbishop did not have full powers and authority of an Archbishop needed to exercise to the fullest extent his authority in such a difficulty and tough situations as was Kenya. Anastasios was simply acting Archbishop. In canonical terms he was answerable to the immediate former Archbishop or in absence of such, he was answerable directly to the then Patriarch as the official exarches of the Archbishopric of Irinoupolis. He did not have the powers to act as he deemed fit on the ground, he needed to ask the higher authorities. Now secondly even with full powers, metropolitans in the Patriarchate of Alexandria are in canonical terms assistants to the patriarch. Archbishop Anastasios was known to have many against him up there in Alexandria who did not like his ways of doing things and he was a minority being from Greece in a climate which was increasingly turning towards the Cypriot winds and whims. Problem number three was Acting Archbishop Anastasios did not give up his professorial job at the University of Athens when he was appointed Acting Archbishop the Archbishopric of Irinoupolis. This was very unfortunate for him since he would be in Kenya only for a few weeks, when he would fly to Kenya only to stay for two to three weeks then fly back to Greece. This mode of work really did him much disservice and harm to his tenure in East Africa. In Kenya, his trusted servant was not a Kenyan of note but a very powerful individual in the person of Archimandrite Jonah Lwanga of Uganda. Jonah, while being a very kind person and a shrewd manager, he did not understand fully the Kenyan cultural dynamics and if he later on did, it was too late for him to be of any help to the Archbishop. Unfortunately, the Archbishop did not see or understand this tribal and national mathematics. This was a very big letdown on the part of the Archbishop and a big short sightedness. Because of the fluid and unpredictable situation in Kenya Archbishop Anastasios should have acted quickly in bring a young man like the powerful Father Paul to his side and made him his Personal Secretary sooner enough, with some power to influence his people. He had the General Secretary Father Eleftherios on his side, but this priest was already a bitter rival of Bishop Gathuna. While he helped the Archbishop tremendously on the political war front, he was cause for much hatred of the Archbishop by the opposition. A sheer lack of a strong and neutral Kenyan leadership in the administration of Archbishop Anastasios proved very costly. At the same time, we need to state in the same breath that father Paul was just coming up as a seminarian and it took the Archbishop a while to get a good grasp of his able character and leadership abilities. Again, Jonah had been trained, since his youth, in the Greek culture of Athens and viewed things from Eastern European mentality and eye rather than African eye, mentality and ear. Due to this lack of the right Kenyan person of some good training, and educated to trust on the ground, a lot of ground was not covered.

Archbishop Anastasios did not have a Kenyan to coordinate his affairs for him on the ground.

When Archbishop Anastasios arrived in Kenya in 1981, he found the mechanisms of Archbishopric of Irinoupolis in place and obeyed the order of the day. Evidence shows that 1st October 1982 Archbishopric of Irinoupolis, through Mrs. Alexandra Contos, wrote a Form 203A, (section 201) of the companies Act (CAP. 486), to the Registrar of Companies notifying them of the change of Directors and Secretaries or in their particulars. The new secretary to the company is listed according to this document, as Mrs. Alexandra Kontos. It also indicates over leaf the names of the council members. According to this document the new council members of Archbishopric of Irinoupolis were: Archbishop Yannoulatos Anastasios, Mr. Tilliridis Andreas, Sister Galini Georgia, Fr. Romeos Anthony and Miss. Kontogeorgi Argro.[254] The same letter of notification has it that Archer and Wilcock were now the new Advocates, representing the Archbishopric of Irinoupolis Company. The nationality of all the directors and secretaries is listed as Greek. That Mrs. Alexandra Contos was also the company secretary of Archbishopric of Irinoupolis is itself very odd considering that Mrs. Alexandra Konontos was also the right-hand Advocate handling the affairs of Archbishopric of Irinoupolis on behalf of Archer and Wilcock Advocates. Certainly, there was conflict of interest here but be it as it may she did represent the company well.

By the time the names of the new officers of the company were sent to the Registrar of Companies, it was discovered that the Archbishopric of Irinoupolis file had disappeared from that office; a new file had to be created.[255] This is common in Kenya especially if a case before the court is political because bribery and other corrupt means of the state

---

[254] Mrs. Alexandra Kontos, for Archbishopric of Irinoupolis Company, to Registrar of Companies, TDS, 1st October 1982.
[255] Mrs. Alexandra Contos, for Archbishopric, Disappearance of the Archbishopric file, to the Assistant registrar of Companies, reference: H / 519 /1 /AK Respectively, TDS, 20th December 1982 and 25th May 1983.

have a way of luring officials into destroying the undesirable files or simply removing them from their right filing order. Such an effort can keep a file afloat and lost for years. I would suspect that probably the file was destroyed by, interests sympathetic to Bishop George Gathuna. In any case, a new file was started and given a new number 13294, which continues to this day to be the official file number of the Archbishopric of Irinoupolis Company in the Registry of Companies.

The most important contribution of Archbishop Anastasios towards solving the problem posed by Archbishopric of Irinoupolis Company was a letter he wrote to the registrar of Companies on 16th May 1986. His letter addressed to the Registrar of Companies, referring to the <u>Change of Name</u>:

> It is the view of the present General Council of the Church that the name "holy Archbishopric of Irinoupolis" is not a clear translation of the name of the Church. The Council has been contemplating to change the name of *Holy Archbishopric of Irinoupolis* to read *Orthodox Archdiocese of East Africa (Holy Archbishopric of Irinoupolis)*.[256]

First let us examine the wording of the letter. The wording of this letter tells us that the Archbishop understood the cultural, commercial, political dynamics and legal problems associated with this name and was under much pressure, one, to conceal as much as he could the reasons for the desired change of the name, and the meaning of the name of the company in Orthodox terms. He was also under great pressure to contain the African insurgence, which was mounting in power and gaining ground in popularity. In September 1986 African priests, succeeded in amending the Constitution of the Greek African Orthodox Church to the original name at the time of foundation which was,

---

[256] Bishop Prof. Anastasios Yanoulatos, Ref: 1649, change of the name of Holy Archbishopric of Irinoupolis, to the Registrar of Companies, TDS, on 16th May 1986.

African Orthodox Church.[257] It also made quite a number of changes in it, one of them being that the church shall be headed or managed by canonically ordained priests (who shall be Kenyans).[258]

Archbishop Anastasios calls the general Council of the company of Irinoupolis, the council of the Church. Why he did that is important because he tried to make it appear that this council and the governing council of the Orthodox Church in Kenya was one and the same thing. This was not the case and the Archbishop new that pretty well. What I make of this is that he was under pressure to conceal the real identity of Archbishopric of Irinoupolis especially from the state. But more importantly the African Orthodox opposition force was mounting against the Archbishopric company. By the end of 1985 African priests had gone to court challenging the legitimacy of Archbishopric of Irinoupolis company's continued acting as a church in Kenya. We mentioned that Africans had revolted against Gathuna for refusing to open the Seminary. Well after Gathuna was defrocked, the canonical African leadership splinter group, regrouped under a delicate and loose alliance of leadership so to speak, comprising of three canonical priests and one uncanonical priest. This group as mentioned earlier, were independent of Gathuna as well as the Archbishopric. By the formation of this nucleus, we now had three Orthodox groups from the Original and legitimated one that was born in 1927-8. The three priests were Rev. Father Peter Nganga Michara who was the then chairman of the priests, Rev. John Ngethe Ngugi the treasurer, and Rev. Father Gerasmos Gachumi that of the secretary. The uncanonical one was Father Nicholas Mukoma Gachigi. It was chaos in all Orthodox Churches in Kiambu, and Nairobi areas.[259] Wars were fought, and blood was

---

[257] O. J. Ngugi (MRS) Asst. Registrar of Societies, confirming the approval of a mended constitution, to the Secretary, African Orthodox Church of Kenya, TDS, 1st September 1986.

[258] The African Orthodox Church of Kenya Constitution and Rules Amendments. Article 2. (B).

[259] Daily Nation News Paper Kenya: Court Warning to Priests, Women In

shed many a times. They were fighting among themselves on one front and on the other they were fighting to remove Archbishop Anastasios. This present situation is what prompted Archbishop Anastasios to try to scramble for some solutions. The reason why Archbishop referred to the director's council of Archbishop as a church council was, I think, to counteract the new council formed by the four priests with the support of the majority of the parishes in Nairobi and seemingly a formidable force, which had access to the resources of the African government at state house. By the end of 1986, African group of priests opposed to both Bishop Gathuna and Archbishop Anastasios, after wrestling with the two in a court of law, managed to get hold of the Certificate of incorporation.[260] With the certificate of incorporation in their hands the formidable four had dislodged the Archbishopric from the certificate of incorporation. Secondly, the Archbishop states "it is not a clear translation of the name of the Church." The group of four priest had managed to put to the state that this was a Greek company and so the Archbishop was at pains to show that his organization was really a church organization. The truth was that the translation and the meaning, activities, and objectives of this company were not and are not even close to the meaning of the word church and so it meant totally something different and thus the need for the archbishop to explain. The memorandum of association of Archbishopric does not and neither does the Articles of association say that Holy Archbishopric is a church but they both say that it is a company. What we read here is that the new Archbishop had his back against the wall. Here he wished to do the right thing under very difficult circumstance and with limited options to maneuver from, seeing that his hands

---

Beatings of Priests, 17, May 1979.
- Daily Nat Church row grows, No.6159, Monday September 22 1980.
[260] Mr. Eliud Timothy Mwamunga Minister for Lands and Settlement Republic of Kenya, Certificate of Incorporation Under the Trustees (Perpetual Succession) Act (chapter 164), to African Orthodox Church, TDS, 22nd September 1986.

were tied from the back by Alexandria. What he calls his church was literally slipping through his fingers. In this document Archbishop Anastasios understood that there was a big problem with this company and that this name Archbishopric had to be removed in order for him to bring peace. He had been in Kenya for over five years now and knew exactly where the problem was situated. It does not necessarily mean that he wanted to completely get rid of it but wanted to a peace Africans by using a more moderate term that would have appeared as a prefix before the actual and real meaningful name. The fact that he intended to have the name of the church read Orthodox Church, Archdiocese of East Africa (Archbishopric of Irinoupolis) shows that he had concern for true representation of the Orthodox faith and concern for the right way of doing church business. It shows his deep understanding of Orthodox situation in Kenya and the problem that Archbishopric Company posed, then and still poses now to the future stability of the Church. For a while people were excited about this move but suddenly all went very quiet and the whole thing died out. We do not know what happened after. The fact that such a high-ranking clergy and Acting Archbishop thought, at the time that the Archbishopric of Irinoupolis was not representative of the real meaning and translation of the word Orthodox Church, gives credence to the African cry that Archbishopric is not a church but a company of a few people.

Since 1986 to the present we have been in and out of court with this case. It does not end, no one side will win unless and until the real problem is dealt with, the Archbishopric of Irinoupolis Company. Divisive structures and names that create animosity should be done away with, and administrative structure reconstructed to fit an ecclesiastically recognizable church order and rules clearly made to accommodate African leadership.

Bibliography and Sources

Agapios & Nicodemos (Eds.) *The Rudder, (Pedalion) of the Metaphorical Ship of the Catholic and Apostolic Church of the Orthodox Christians,* Translation by D. Cummings, Published by The Orthodox Christian Educational Society, Chicago Illinois 1957.

Anderson William. B., *The Church In East Africa 1840 – 1974,* (Dodoma, Tanzania: Uzima CTP CPH, 1977).

Barret David B., Schism and Renewal in Africa, (Nairobi: Oxford University Press, 1968).

Berman Bruce, *Control & Crisis in Colonial Kenya,* (London: James Curry, 1990).

Bogololepov Alexander, *Towards An American Orthodox Church,* (New York: SVS Press, 1963).

Cone James H., God of The Oppressed, (New York: The Seabury Press, 1975).

Edgerton Robert B., *Mau Mau An African Crucible,* (n. p, Free press 1989).

Erickson John H., *The Challenge of Our Past,* (Crestwood New York: St. Vladimir's Seminary 1991).

Huxley Elspeth and Margery Perham, *Race And Politics In Kenya.* (London: Faber and Paber LTD. Mcmxliv)

_____.Huxley Elspeth, *White Man's Country1914-130,* vol. II, (n. p.)

Johnson Walton R., *Worship And Freedom,* (New York: African Publishing Company, 1977).

Linden Ian & Jane Linden, *The Church and Revolution in Rwanda*, (Nairobi: African Publishing Company 1977).

Leaky L. S. B., *Defeating Mau Mau.* (London: Methuen LTD, 1955).

Maneo A. Afonso, *What is the Nature of Authority in the Church?* (n. p., University press of America, 1996).

Mandela Nelson Rolihlahla, *Long Walk to Freedom*, (Boston: Little, Brown and Company 1994).

Marpherson R., *The Presbyterian Church in Kenya*, (Nairobi: Presb. Church of E. Africa 1970).

Meredith Martin, *Nelson Mandela, A Biography*, (New York: St. Martins Press 1994).

Mbiti John S., *African Religion and Philosophy.* Second Edition, (Oxford: Heinemann Educational Publishers1989).

_____. *"African Traditional Religions,"* International Review of Mission vol. LIX (1970).

Mercouri Melina, *I was born Greek*, (New York: Dell Publishing Company 1971).

Miller Norman N. *Kenya: The Quest For Prosperity.* (n. p., Westview Press, 1984).

Nthamburi Zablon, *The African Church at the Crossroads, A strategy for Indigenization*, (Nairobi: Uzima Press 1991).

_____. *A History of the Methodist Church in Kenya*, (Nairobi: Uzima Press 1982).

_____. Ed. *From Mission To Church*, (Nairobi: Uzima Press 1991)

Oliver Roland & J. D. Fage, *A Short History of Africa*, (Maryland: Penguin Books Baltimore, 1962).

Petersen Douglas. The Formations of Popular, National, Autonomous Pentecostal Churches in Central America. PNEUMA: *The Journal of the Society for Pentecostal Studies*, Vol. 16, No. 1, Spring (1994).

Philip H. R. A. *A New Day in Kenya*. World Dominion Press, 1936.

Sangree Walter H., Age, Prayer and Politics in Triki, Kenya, (London: Oxford University Press, 1966).

Schaff Philip & Henry Wace. *Seven Ecumenical Councils. Nicene And Post Nicene Fathers*, Second Edition, Vol. XIV. WM. B. Eerdmans Publishing Company Grand Rapid Michigan 1974.

Tuma Tom A. D., *Building A Ugandan Church*, (Nairobi: Kenya Literature Bureau 1980).

_____.& Phares Mutibwa,Ed., *A Century of Christianity in Uganda, 1877-1977*, (n. p , 1978).

Weigert Stephen L., Traditional Religion and Guerrilla Warfare in Modern Africa. *Bureau of Intelligence and Research*, (London: Macmillan Press 1960).

Patsavos Professor Lewis J. *Manual for the Course in Orthodox Canon Law*, (Brookline Massachusetts, 1975).

Sahlberg Carl-Erik. From Krapf to Rugambwa, *A Church History of Tanzania*, (Evangelical Publishing House, Nairobi. 1986).

Shorter Aylward W. F. *African Culture & the Church*, (Orbis Books 1974).

Welbourn. F. B., *East African Rebels*. A Study of Some Independent Churches, (London: SCM Press LTD, 1961).

_____Welbourn F. B., *Religion And Politics in Uganda 1952-1962*, (Nairobi: East African Publishing House, 1965)

_____ Welbourn F. B., & B. A. Ogot, A *Place To Feel at Home*, (Nairobi: Oxford University Press, 1966).

Welch F. G., *Towards An African Church*, (Nairobi: Christian Council of Kenya, 1962).

Wanjau Gakaara, Agikuyu, *Mau Mau Na Wiyathi*, (Nairobi: Thomson Press (1970) LTD, 1971).

Anita Stauffer S., *International Review of Missions vol.* LXXXV 337(1996).

Cotsonis Jeronimos, "The Validity Of The Anglican Orders According To Canon Law Of The Orthodox Church" *Greek Orthodox Theological Review* 3 (1957).

Horner Norman A. An East African Orthodox Church. *The Journal of Ecumenical Studies vol.* 12, Spring (1975).

Karmiris John. "Ways Of Accepting Non-Orthodox Into The Orthodox Church" *Greek Orthodox Theological Review* 1 (1954).

Schmemann Alexander, *Problems of Orthodoxy in America*, SVS 8 # 2 (1963).

Booth Newell Snow, "Mission Priorities in Africa", *International Review of Mission Vol.* 37 (1948)

Orthodox Word, Orthodox Mission Today: "The African Orthodox Church", July – August (1968).

Ware Kallistos Bishop. The light that Enlightens Everyone: The Knowledge of God among the Non-Christians According to the Greek fathers and St. Innocent, *The Greek Orthodox Theological Review* Vol. 44 Number 1-4, (1999).

Wentink D. E., "The Orthodox Church in East Africa", *The Ecumenical Review* vol. 20, WCC, January – December (1968)

Patsavos Lewis J., History of the Greek Orthodox Church in America, Miltiades B. Efthimiou and George A. Christopoulos, Ed. (New York: Greek Archdiocese, 1984), p. 67.

Charter of The Greek Orthodox Archdiocese of North And South America, TDS, (Brookline, Mass HCO Press, 1978).

Owen Archdeacon, to C.M.S. Secretary, Nairobi, March 23 1923 (C.M.S. Archives Nairobi).

His Grace Bishop Gathuna, to His Holiness Ecumenical Patriarch Demetrios, TDS, 1 st. March 1980.

Daily Nation –Kenya Newspaper No.6159, Monday, September 22, 1980, p.1.

Archbishopric of Irinoupolis to Kenyan Government Company Act (cap. 486), Memorandum of Association, The Name of the Company (hereinafter called "the Archbishopric), TDS, 29 January 1968.

Minutes of a meeting of the General Council of the Holy Archbishopric of Irinoupolis held at the offices of Messrs. Hamilton Harrison & Matthews, Nairobi on the 30th September1974, P. 1-2. DS

Attorney Generals office Nairobi to Archbishopric of Irinoupolis, The Companies Act (CAP. 486) License pursuant to section 21(1), DS, 8 November 1967.

Memorandum of Association of Holy Archbishopric of Irinoupolis, Part 3, The objects for which the Archbishopric of Irinoupolis is established, section (A) (1 - 3), DS, 29 January 1968, p. 1.

The Companies Memorandum and Articles of Association of Holy Archbishopric of Irinoupolis, to the Companies Act (cap. 486) of the Republic of Kenya at Nairobi, DS, 7th.February 1968.

Mr. Andrew In Anthony Warwick, For Archbishopric Company, to Registrar of Companies, DS, January 1968.

O. J. Burns, Assistant Registrar of Companies, Certificate of Incorporation, to Archbishopric of Irinoupolis, DS, 20th February 1968.

Archimandrite Chrysostomos Papassarantopoulos, to Registrar of Companies, DS, 24th. January1968.

Directors and Subscribers to Archbishopric, Articles of Association, DS, 29th. January 1968, p.16.

Registrar General of the Department of Registry of Companies, to Archbishopric of Irinoupolis, TDS, 17th May 1972.

Eminence Archbishop Nicodemos, for Archbishopric, to the Registrar General Registry of Companies Nairobi, TDS, 3rd July 1972

Assistant Registrar of Companies, to Mr. Kithyomi, TDS, 5thJuly 1974.

Minutes of the General Council of the Holy Archbishopric of Irinou-polis, held at the offices of Messrs. Hamilton Harrison & Matthews Nairobi, TDS, 30th September1974, pp.1-2.

Attorney Generals office, The Companies Act (CAP. 486), License Pur-suant to Section 21(1) of the Government of Kenya, TDS, 8th. November1967.

Minutes of the General Council of the Holy Archbishopric of Irinou-polis, held at the offices of Messrs. Hamilton Harrison & Matthews Nairobi, TDS, 30th September1974, pp.1-2.

Extraordinary meeting of the Holy Archbishopric of Irinoupolis Nai-robi, TDS, 16th October 1974

General meeting of the Holy Archbishopric of Irinoupolis Nairobi held immediately following the extraordinary one, TDS, 16th Octo-ber 1974.

Assistant Registrar of Companies, to M/S. Hamilton Harrison & Mat-thews Advocates, copied to the Directors of Holy Archbishopric of Irinoupolis, Nairobi, TDS, 15th November1974.

The state verses Archbishopric of Irinoupolis, The Resident Magistrates Court Nairobi, Criminal Case No. 320, TDS, 30[th]July 1974.

The Deputy Registrar General of the registry of Companies, to C. R. O. (Mr. Sameja), TDS, 7th November1974.

Assistant Registrar of Companies, file Ref: C.13294, to Hamilton Harrison & Matthews Advocate, for Archbishopric of Irinoupolis, TDS, on 15th March 1975.

Assistant Registrar of Companies, Ref: C.13294, to Hamilton Harrison & Matthews Advocate, for the Company of Archbishopric of Irinoupolis, TDS, 4th February 1975.

Archbishop Anastasios was acting Archbishop of East Africa from 1981-1991.

Mrs. Alexandra Kontos, for Archbishopric of Irinoupolis Company, to Registrar of Companies, TDS, 1st October 1982.

Mrs. Alexandra Contos, for Archbishopric, Disappearance of the Archbishopric file, to the Assistant registrar of Companies, reference: H / 519 /1 /AK Respectively, TDS, 20th December 1982 and 25th May 1983.

Bishop Prof. Anastasios Yanoulatos, Ref: 1649, change of the name of A Holy Archbishopric of Irinoupolis, to the Registrar of Companies, TDS, on 16th May 1986.

O. J. Ngugi (MRS) Asst. Registrar of Societies, confirming the approval of a mended constitution, to the Secretary, African Orthodox Church of Kenya, TDS, 1st September1986.

The African Orthodox Church of Kenya Constitution and Rules Amendments. Article 2. (B).

The African Orthodox Church of Kenya Constitution and Rules Amendments. Article 2. (B).

Mr. Eliud Timothy Mwamunga Minister for Lands and Settlement Republic of Kenya, Certificate of Incorporation Under the Trustees (Perpetual Succession) Act (chapter 164), to African Orthodox Church, TDS, 22nd September 1986.

Daily Nation News Paper Kenya: Court Warning to Priests, Women In Beatings of Priests, 17, May 1979.

Daily Nation News Paper, Church row grows, No.6159, Monday, September 22, 1980.

The Hellenic Voice, newspaper, Wednesday, August 1, 2001.

Walker Adrian, A Believer's Rude Reward, The Boston Globe Monday August 20, 2001.

ABOUT THE AUTHOR

The Very Rev. Dr. Archimandrite Anastasios, Elekiah Andago Kihali, (M.Div., Th.M, PhD) is a Kenyan Orthodox archimandrite priest serving in the Church of Kenya. He is a graduate of our Holy Cross Greek Orthodox School of Theology. He also graduated from St Makarios Patriarchal Seminary in Nairobi, as well as receiving a Doctor of Theology in Missiology from the Aristotle University of Thessalonica. He served as a missionary in Albania for three years under Archbishop Anastasios, his spiritual father, and has been serving in his home country of Kenya since 2010. He is presently the Dean of Embu in the Orthodox Diocese of Nyeri and Mount Kenya Region. In 2018, he established the St. Paul's Godjope Hills Academy and Orphanage, an Elementary and Middle School in Migori County, Western Kenya, which presently has 150 students, of which 50 receive scholarships to attend. Elekiah Andago Kihali is the sixth of 10 children of Mzee Hosea Kihali and the late Mama Peris Gweyani Kihali:

Elekiah Andago Kihali

Here is a brief autobiography of Fr. Kihali:

"I taught secondary school before joining St. Makarios Patriarchal Seminary 1986 and graduated at the top in 1989. I was offered a scholarship by the Very Reverend Fr. Alexander Veronis as president of OCMC in collaboration with Holy Cross Greek School of Theology at the kind request of His Beatitude Archbishop Anastasios of Tirana and all Albania (then the Archbishop of East Africa and Kenya). I arrived at Hellenic College/Holy Cross in February, 1990. There I took undergraduate classes before joining Holy Cross for the Master of Divinity; I graduated in 1993 with distinction. In 1994 I enrolled at Holy Cross for a Master of Theology (Th.M.) degree and at the same time enrolled for the Doctor of Theology (Th.D.) at Boston University. In 1995 I was part of small group of young men and women who left the Diocese of Boston under the Leadership of the Very Reverend Fr. Ted Barbas for Tijuana Mexico to build a home for a needy poor family in Mexico. I did class work at both schools, Holy Cross and Boston, but due to financial constraints both efforts were left incomplete.

I then returned to Africa and proceeded to Albania in summer of 1996 (sent by OCMC) to serve as a missionary teacher. At Holy Resurrection Seminary at St. Vlash I taught Preaching and Canon Law! My missionary tour ended in October 1998 and I returned to Kenya to teach at St. Makarios Seminary, my former school. On April 4th of that year, by the grace of God, I was ordained to the rank of Deacon and given the revered name of my Spiritual Father, Anastasios. In the same month on April 16th, I was elevated to the Holy Priesthood, and on May 9th became an Archimandrite with blessing if Metropolitan Seraphim Kykotis. In 2000, while teaching 'Preaching, Canon Law and Missions' at St. Makarios, I earned the title of Senior Lecturer from Metropolitan Seraphim (then Archbishop of Kenya and now the Archbishop of Zimbabwe). In 2001, I was offered a scholarship by then President of Hellenic College Holy Cross the Very Reverend Fr. Nicholas

Triantafilou to return at Holy Cross to finish my thesis for the Theology Master (Th.M.) degree in History and Canon Law under the Direction of Professor Fr. Tom Fitzgerald and Professor James Skedros. I graduated in 2002 with high Distinction and my copyrighted Thesis is entitled "*Challenges facing the Orthodox Church Movements in East Africa. From 1928 to the Present.*"

In July of 2002, I returned to Kenya and was assigned to Kampala, Uganda to assist Metropolitan Jonah Lwanga and teacher at St. Paul's Seminary. My mission tour in Uganda ended in 2004 when again, by the gracious and generous offer of His Beatitude Archbishop Anastasios, via the assistance of Metropolitan Jonah and Professor Dimitra Koukoura, I was offered a scholarship at The University of Aristotle Thessaloniki to study Greek Language and to do a doctorate of Philosophy in the History of Missiology. I graduated in June 2009 with the Doctor of Philosophy (PhD) and returned to Kenya summer of 2009, where I served as the General Vicar of Western Kenya Bishoprics. I am currently the Dean of Embu in the Orthodox Diocese of Nyeri and Mount region Kenya."

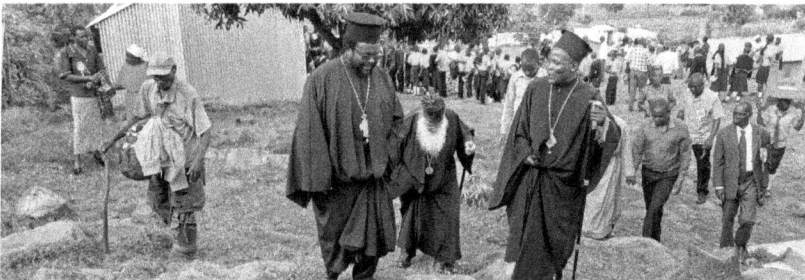

www.ingramcontent.com/pod-product-compliance
Lightning Source LLC
Chambersburg PA
CBHW071807090426
42737CB00012B/1991